Sagittarius

23 November – 22 December

About
Dadhichi

Dadhichi is one of Australia's foremost astrologers, and is frequently seen on TV and in the media. He has the unique ability to draw from complex astrological theory to provide clear, easily understandable advice and insights for people who want to know what their future may hold.

In the 25 years that Dadhichi has been practising astrology, and conducting face and other esoteric readings, he has provided over 9,000 consultations. His clients include celebrities, political and diplomatic figures and media and corporate identities from all over the world.

Dadhichi's unique blend of astrology and face reading helps people fulfil their true potential. His extensive experience practising western astrology is complemented by his research into the theory and practice of eastern forms of astrology.

Dadhichi has been a guest on many Australian television shows and several of his political and worldwide forecasts have proved uncannily accurate. He has appeared on many of Australia's leading television networks and is a regular columnist for several Australian magazines.

His websites www.astrology.com.au, www.facereader.com and soulmate.com.au which attract hundreds of thousands of visitors each month, offer a wide variety of features, helpful information and services.

Welcome from
Dadhichi

Dear Friend,

It's a pleasure knowing you're reading this, your astrological forecast for 2009. There's nothing more exciting than looking forward to a bright new year and considering what the stars have in store and how you might make the most of what's on offer in your life.

Apart from the anticipation of what I might predict will happen to you, of what I say about your upcoming luck and good fortune, remember that astrology is first and foremost a tool of personal growth, self-awareness and inner transformation. What 'happens to us' is truly a reflection of what we're giving out; the signals we are transmitting to our world, our universe.

The astrological adage of 'As above, so below' can also be interpreted in a slightly different way when I say 'As within, so without'! In other words, as hard as it is to believe, the world and our experiences of it, or our relationships and circumstances, good or bad, do tend to mirror our own belief systems and mental patterns.

It is for this reason that I thought I'd write a brief introductory note to remind you that the stars are pointers to your wonderful destiny and that you must work with them to realise your highest and most noble goals. The greatest marvel and secret is your own inner self! Astrology reveals these inner secrets of your character, which are the foundation of your life's true purpose.

What is about to happen to you this year is exciting, but what you *do* with this special power of knowledge, how you share your talents with others, and the way you truly enjoy

Contents

The best things in life aren't things.

—Anonymous

Sagittarius: A Snapshot

Key characteristics

Magnanimous, honest, expansive, generous, reckless,
extroverted, proud, larger than life, free

Compatible star signs

Aries, Leo, Libra, Aquarius

Key life phrase

I expand

Life goals

To explore the world and grow in understanding

Platinum assets

Fearlessness, optimism and goodwill

Zodiac totem

The Centaur

Zodiac symbol

♐

Zodiac facts

Ninth sign of the zodiac; mutable, barren, masculine, dry

Jupiter is responsible for your luck but you do have a tendency to believe nothing will go wrong, and for this reason you're known as being a bit of a risk taker as well. Friends and family members may be frightened by this attitude but they secretly envy you for having such a strong belief in yourself.

You're a big thinker in everything you do and can't handle any response like, 'Oh, you can't do that', or 'That'll never work out'. You must surround yourself with people who believe that they can achieve things and mutually you'll be able to help each other achieve those farsighted goals.

'The bigger, the better' seems to be the Sagittarian trademark and you're happy to take a shot at anything you believe is worthwhile. No one is going to stop you once you've made up your mind.

You have an incredible sense of timing, which means you often find yourself in the right place at just the right time to make things happen for you. You also have an uncanny knack of hooking up with people who can help you achieve your ambitions.

You're very interested in personal growth and self-understanding, which is part of the other Sagittarian ideal of expansion. Expanding your horizons is what you are about and any knowledge, philosophy or facts and figures that can give you a deeper and broader insight into life is perfect for you.

Getting to the bottom of things and understanding why life is the way it is fascinates you and therefore you need to associate with others who can act as catalysts for your journey of knowledge. You will make many pilgrimages to different parts of the globe in your search for self-understanding and, in fact, your whole life is one big pilgrimage in your quest for self-knowledge.

Three classes of Sagittarius

If you are born between the 23rd of November and the 2nd of December you are a true Sagittarian and will exhibit the traits mentioned here in full. Always optimistic and ready for an adventure, life will be full of pleasure and unexpected good fortune.

If your birth date falls between the 3rd and the 12th of December, fiery Mars and Aries as well as Sagittarius rule you. You are a spicier and more hot-tempered class of Sagittarian and are always on the go but can also get yourself into hot water with your impulsive nature. Physical by nature, sports will be an important component of keeping yourself stable and peaceful.

The third group of Sagittarians born between the 13th and the 22nd of December are co-ruled by the Sun and Leo. The majestic royal solar energies endow you with an incredibly strong sense of self and also the likelihood of tremendous success personally and financially. You will also develop a more spiritual attitude as you get older.

Sagittarius role model: Brad Pitt

Brad Pitt exhibits the bold and adventurous traits of your Sagittarian nature. Apart from the wonderfully successful film career he has enjoyed, we see his humanitarian empathy shining through his activities with and marriage to Angelina Jolie and their adoption of several children from different cultures.

Sagittarius: The light side

Nothing can keep a Sagittarian down and being the supreme optimist, you're able to get up repeatedly when life beats you around the ears, as it is does from time to time. Unlike others, you realise there is no point in complaining and always try to see what's happening to you in the best possible light.

And, finally, try not to over-exaggerate your stories. People will trust and appreciate you much more.

Sagittarius woman

In a Sagittarian woman you'll find the most wonderful blend of optimism and femininity. The loving and compassionate energy of Jupiter are always obvious in you and this expresses itself as affection and joy. You make friends easily because of this and your unique brand of enthusiasm and energy also tends to make you seductive to members of the opposite sex.

You're a straight shooter; you shoot straight from the hip and have a down-to-earth attitude even though you're in touch with the spiritual and subtle aspects of life. You do have a tendency to want to see the best in life and people and, as long as you can balance this with the practicality of day-to-day life, you can be the ideal dreamer who does manifest these dreams in the world and do so without becoming a recluse or an airhead.

The element of humour is strong in your character and is one of the personality traits that will take you far. Although you have a great sense of wit, your integrity is still the cornerstone of your personality, so everyone knows they can rely on you and you are honest. Actually, you are too honest and at times this comes across as bluntness; but you prefer to call a spade a spade rather than lead people on and give them a false sense of security.

Intimidation is not a feature of your character that stands out; however, in your desire to be right, you may sometimes appear to be a little overpowering with your high level of con- fidence. You must understand that the average person doesn't have the same degree of energy and optimism as you do and this can be a little daunting to them, especially on first meeting you.

Other women can sometimes feel uncomfortable in your presence because you don't play the prissy, plastic-manufactured female game. You're the 'real deal' and this can often highlight the pretentiousness of others. This again reflects your extremely forthright nature. Your intuition is strong in this respect and you can sense deceit a mile away. You're very good at uncovering the truth and telling as it is.

You'll have a large circle of acquaintances but not always that many close friends because even those who hang out with you secretly feel you are a little arrogant. You just like to share every part of your being with everyone and this is something that is foreign to the average person on the street.

Throughout your life your successes will attract envy and the odd enemy, but you'll brush these people aside and not make too much of it. You have bigger fish to catch and yet again your optimism is tied in with your philosophy of not letting yourself be dragged down to the lowest common denominator.

You have an extremely big heart and are very compassionate. You like to help others and as a friend you'll go beyond the call of duty to make sure that a person's suffering is lessened. You mustn't let others take advantage of your good nature, however. It won't be the first time that a Sagittarian girl has fallen for a hard luck story and been taken for a ride.

Not many people are able to laugh at themselves but you've developed this part of your character sufficiently enough to make sure that you journey through life will be much easier and certainly more fun.

Finally, Jupiter, your ruler, is the lucky one and will certainly gift you with the right circumstances and ultimately the right people to fulfil your life.

Sagittarius man

Positive thinking, abundant energy and gregarious humour are the tripod upon which the Sagittarian male personality rests. With such incredible energy infusing your Sagittarian being,

You have a great way of communicating ideas and are probably one of the more honest signs of the zodiac. You need to sweeten the truth, however, because at times your manner cuts straight to the crux of the matter and can often wound the sensitivities of those who are less resilient.

You have a wonderful ability to treat all people equally. You have an eclectic way dealing with people and with culture and philosophical views. You like to see yourself as the torch-bearer for accommodating all people's views and philosophies.

As a husband and father you'll bring much joy to your family and can be a great role model to your children. Actually, many Sagittarian men never cease to be big kids at heart themselves!

Sagittarius child

I hope you have plenty of room in your home if the child you've brought into this world was born under the sign of Sagittarius. Bundles of energy that never stop and who need ample space to express their wild and wonderful antics will be essential if they are to grow up feeling fulfilled.

Hearty laughter is their signature and, if you can't quite pinpoint where they are at any given moment, just move in the direction of where the laughter is coming from. That's where you'll find your Sagittarian child.

Sagittarian kids are wonderfully kind and generous and this makes them popular, even in the early stages of their schooling.

They need to be in an environment that allows them to wander and explore the local terrain. Being adventurous by nature these little daredevils need to ferret out and discover all aspects of their environment. Give them plenty of space to investigate the world and this part of their personality. You'll note from day one that your Sagittarian infant is extremely

You have optimism about relationships and believe that you're destined to meet someone who can meet your expectations romantically. Being a fire sign you are passionate and have a natural inclination for romance and sex so if there is anyone else out there up to the challenge you're more than happy to invite them to step into the ring of fire, and go forward with you to enjoy life.

Some Sagittarians tend to see relationships as a never-ending challenge and can hop, skip and jump from one partner to another, never feeling fully settled. If you are excited or passionate about someone you're with, the gloss can sometimes rub off fairly quickly if they are not as upbeat and animated as yourself. Try to extend your philosophical view of life and look a little deeper into the person's character before making hasty judgements about them.

Sport and play are essential for you in love as they are in life. You need partners born under the star signs that can give you mental and physical stimulation and in particular the air signs of Gemini, Libra and Aquarius will do that (see the compatibility sections for the interpretation on how these star signs work for you).

You have a very amorous nature but at times are hot and fiery, so much so that your search for passion can overstimulate you to such an extent that you miss out on any emotional satisfaction. Don't overlook the subtler aspects of the relationship and what that person has to offer you. Again, try to look below the surface if you are looking for long-time satisfaction in a relationship.

There are times when a Sagittarian will finally realise that the sexual excitement of a relationship in no way fulfils the broader requirements of the Sagittarian character. It's true that you need a deeper mental connection with your lover if you are to feel contentment in the long term.

mental attitude, and science and medicine have now proved this is an excellent antidote for disease and other physical problems.

Because you love exercise and outdoor activities it's likely you'll have plenty of fresh air and lots of physical movement to also augment your state of good health.

This optimistic mental attitude will bring you good luck and wonderful health right into your old age and, as with most of us, if you do happen to have the odd physical problem you have remarkable recuperative powers, so don't worry.

Sagittarius has rulership over the thighs and hip area and this includes the pelvis and lower back. Constitutionally these are the weak points. Because Taurus also regulates the health of Sagittarius, your neck, throat and upper shoulders can also give you the occasional bit of trouble. Regular massages and yoga will help keep these parts of your body flexible and in good working condition.

Food can become a problem for some Sagittarians who have a tendency to gain weight with age. This reflects a lack of willpower when it comes to rich foods and fine dining. You should eat smaller meals more regularly and of course try to burn off those excess calories through exercise.

The old adage 'Eat like a king in the morning, like a prince at midday, and a pauper at night' is the saying all Sagittarians should commit to memory and apply to their dietary habits. Stay away from high-carbohydrate foods, particularly later in the day and into the night. As your metabolism slows down towards the end of the day, you are less able to burn off those high-packed calories.

The best foods for Sagittarius are vegetables, lentils, broccoli, olives and the greener leafy vegetables. These vegetables have all the nutrients, vitamins and minerals your body needs. If you must eat meat, try to avoid the high-fat meats

Gravitation is not responsible for people falling in love.

—Albert Einstein

Romantic compatibility

How compatible are you with your current partner, lover or friend? Did you know that astrology can reveal a whole new level of understanding between people simply by looking at their star sign and that of their partner? In this chapter I'd like to share some special insights that will help you better appreciate your strengths and challenges using Sun sign compatibility.

The Sun reflects your drive, willpower and personality. The essential qualities of two star signs blend like two pure colours, producing an entirely new colour. Relationships, similarly, produce their own emotional colours when two people interact. The following is a general guide to your romantic prospects with others and how, by knowing the astrological 'colour' of each other, the art of love can help you create a masterpiece.

When reading the following I ask you to remember that no two star signs are ever *totally* incompatible. With effort and compromise, even the most 'difficult' astrological matches can work. Don't close your mind to the full range of life's possibilities! Learning about each other and ourselves is the most important facet of astrology.

Each star sign combination is followed by the elements of those star signs and the result of their combining. For instance, Aries is a fire sign and Aquarius is an air sign, and this combination produces a lot of 'hot air'. Air feeds fire, and fire warms air. In fact, fire requires air. However, not all air and fire combinations work. I have included information about the different birth periods within each star sign and this will throw even more light on your prospects for a fulfilling love life with any star sign you choose.

Quick reference guide: Horoscope compatibility between signs (percentage)

	Pisces	Aquarius	Capricorn	Sagittarius	Scorpio	Libra	Virgo	Leo	Cancer	Gemini	Taurus	Aries
Aries	65	55	50	90	80	70	45	90	65	65	65	60
Taurus	85	80	95	50	85	75	90	70	80	70	70	60
Gemini	50	90	50	75	60	90	75	80	60	75	70	70
Cancer	90	70	45	55	95	60	75	70	75	60	80	65
Leo	75	70	45	95	75	65	75	85	70	80	70	90
Virgo	70	50	95	70	85	80	70	75	75	75	90	45
Libra	50	95	85	80	85	80	80	65	60	90	75	70
Scorpio	95	60	65	80	90	85	85	75	95	60	85	80
Sagittarius	75	60	55	85	85	80	70	95	55	75	50	90
Capricorn	85	70	85	55	65	85	95	45	45	50	95	50
Aquarius	55	80	70	60	60	95	50	70	70	90	80	55
Pisces	80	55	85	75	95	50	70	75	90	50	85	65

is the most practical and down-to-earth of signs and may like to live in what you consider too much of a compartmentalised bubble. You on the other hand like the excitement and spontaneity of life and are happy, at least most of the time, not to have too much structure or routine to your lifestyle.

You love to live on the cutting edge and because of this Taureans will feel a little unsettled. Their need for the predictable could cause you some concern. They could see your adventurous lifestyle as a threat to their security and, particularly where money is concerned, you may experience considerable differences.

Socialising will be important to both of you but you have a more direct and lively sort of temperament and Taurus is more cautious in his or her choice of friends. Living an unstructured life is quite contrary to the predictable sort of lifestyle that Taurus is accustomed to. You don't want to get yourself stuck in a rut just as they don't want to move ahead as creatively or spontaneously as you.

Essentially you are a more adaptable creature than Taurus and therefore the key words of your relationships are going to be compromise and adaptability. It is going to take some time for these to develop so adjusting to each other's lifestyle will help the relationship immensely.

You must understand that Taurus is a stubborn sort of bull and no amount of pushing can cause them to change their mind or their ways, irrespective of how rational your ideas may be.

Your sexual experience with Taurus can be good; even though your ruling planets are not particularly friendly, they do provide you a wealth of sensitivity and caring.

Taureans have a need for family and settled life so once you're prepared to assure them that this too is what you want, your relationship can really take off. But, you will have to be a little more patient and perseverant with them.

Taureans born between 21 and 29 April aren't really that compatible with you. The double-influence of Venus means your own health can be affected by being in a relationship if you're not able to slow down and adapt yourself to their demands. This can be a frustrating relationship.

You're quite well suited to Taureans born between 30 April and 10 May. Although this is only marginally better than the last group of Taureans, you'll be stimulated by their intellectual ways and your communication will be a strong point for you. If you do choose to commit to each other, this relationship has a chance of surviving.

Financial issues will make or break your relationship with any Taurean born between 11 and 21 May. Saturn and Capricorn have a strong influence over them so they are the most practical of the Taureans. Financial and professional life together will be an important component of your romance.

SAGITTARIUS + GEMINI
Fire + Air = Hot Air

When star signs of a fiery nature combine with star signs of air, we have a very combustible combination and this is precisely what will happen with Sagittarius and Gemini.

Don't be surprised to cross the path of a Gemini at some point in your life because this is quite a karmic relationship and one very well suited to triggering your romantic and sexual feelings for each other.

You are both very changeable characters by nature so variety will be the spice of life for you together. You'll be physically, mentally and generally very active and this will constitute the core of your mutual satisfaction.

Being on the go, travelling, meeting others while exploring life and the many characters that these situations bring with them, will inspire you both as a couple. You may both in fact choose to travel and live in other countries due to your strong desire for cultural variety as well.

There is one drawback I see in this combination, which is your personalities are so changeable that making decisions and becoming practical about life could be very delayed, if it happens at all. You will both want to sow your wild oats and get rid of the travel itch before you make a firm commitment to settle down and have a family.

Your sexual relationship with a Gemini is excellent because Gemini is a thoroughly intellectual and inventive sign. You may well apply these unique traits of character to their intimate relationship with you and you will absolutely love this. Air and fire naturally warm and accentuate each other's qualities and so there will be a lot of sensual and emotional exchange between you, leading to an exciting relationship physically.

Good times are ahead if you team up with a Gemini born between 22 May and 1 June. You have an immediate attraction for these types on every level of their being. Your desires can be fulfilled with them and there does seem to be a very good synchronicity—socially and domestically—between you.

With Geminis born between 2 and 12 June there could be some confusion surrounding their personalities. It's not a bad idea to develop a friendship with them first before tying yourself down emotionally or sexually. You might want a more intense relationship with them but the mercurial nature of Gemini could mean you are waiting a while before they commit to you. Work on the friendship.

Geminis born between 13 and 21 June are highly strung individuals. You like this 'buzz' on one level but it could frazzle your nerves as well. They have flashes of mental brilliance and intuition, which, when mixed with a great sense of humour, will never leave you bored or wanting for excitement. These people do have a tendency to take on too much and this is probably one aspect of their personality that needs some work. If you yourself are a livewire, this could be a relationship that explodes for a while and then burns out.

SAGITTARIUS + CANCER
Fire + Water = Steam

You couldn't find two more diametrically opposed star signs as Sagittarius and Cancer. You, on the one hand, being larger than life, outgoing and adventure seeking, are really very different to Cancer, the water sign, which is sensitive, soft and intuitive. Yet strangely there is still a unique kind of attraction between your star signs given that your ruling planet, Jupiter, and theirs, the Moon, are friendly in the planetary portfolio.

Cancer appears to be much hardier than it is. They're actually sensitive and thin-skinned individuals who will take your brutally honest statements to heart. They'll never let you know, however, and you will continue to interact with them on exactly the same level without ever knowing just how much you are offending or hurting them. This is where you will need to develop your own sensitivity and observe the body language of Cancer to learn what is going on in their hearts and minds.

Cancer has a tendency to sometimes hide their feelings but your element of fire has the ability to draw them out of themselves, warm the cockles of their heart and share their inner feelings with you. This too is not a bad talent to have with Cancer and will help secure the relationship, taking it to a deeper and more productive level.

Cancer is a domestic sign, naturally attracted to family and domestic life and they will need to know that you too want to have a family with a genuine desire to support them in that goal.

Cancer is one of the more sensual zodiac signs so it's quite likely a considerable amount of passion will be sparked with your relationship with them. Don't forget that Cancer is an emotional sign and will never stand for any physicality of a brutish nature.

Be prepared to take the lows with the highs if you enter into a relationship with Cancer born between the 22 June and 3 July. Cancer is generally sensitive but this bunch is hyper-sensitive and you may need to adjust yourself to this fact. Tone down your extravagant gestures, too, as this could unsettle them. They are a practical type of character.

There is a natural attraction to Cancers born between 4 and 13 July, but you should move slowly before committing yourself to them. Issues of family history, culture and possibly even philosophical viewpoints may be a stumbling block in the way of a successful relationship with them. Get the thumbs up on these important issues before making that all-important commitment.

There's an ease and comfort you feel with Cancers born between 14 and 22 July. You resonate well with them and can have a happy life if you choose to settle down with them.

Great social prospects and exciting romantic indulgences will be yours with Cancer but you mustn't close your mind to the fact that they require some extra tender loving care due to their sensitive nature.

SAGITTARIUS + LEO
Fire + Fire = Explosion

It's an obvious fact that when fire joins with fire an explosion usually occurs. Likewise, the relationship between Sagittarius and Leo can be one that is warming and endearing to both or explosive in the extreme. The choice is yours.

With your straightforward attitude and Leo's arrogance, you could find yourselves running headlong into each other and then spending inordinate amounts of time trying to disentangle yourselves from the problems you create together. This might be one of the karmic lessons you have come to meet. You will need to learn how to speak your mind without sounding as if you are a know-it-all and for Leo to humble themselves and not feel as if they are always right as well.

Because you are so honest, you forget that others aren't able to deal with the truth as easily as you can. Leo is so proud that there is a risk your harsh statements could inflict a deep and irreparable wound. Leo doesn't forget that easily. You must let them feel as if they are the master for the most part because this is the nature of their totem, the lion, the king of the jungle.

Leos need to listen more without reacting too strongly. Once they tune in to your honesty they'll realise that what you have to say comes from your heart.

You appreciate the fact that Leo is as enthusiastic and energetic as you are in virtually everything they do. Passion is part of their nature and although you are more easygoing than your Leo partner the intuitive understanding between you seems to be a bridge that can lessen the gap between your differences.

Both of you are spontaneous, fresh and creative in your love life. Your physical connection will be a great and loving one and will actually augment your health. Again, sexually this is probably one of the best combinations in the zodiac.

A wonderful destiny awaits you with a Leo born between 24 July and 4 August because the Sun and Leo rule your higher learning. You can learn so much from these individuals that your relationship will not be anchored only to the physical but indicates a tremendous amount of spiritual growth as well.

It would be like looking in a mirror with Leos born between 5 and 14 August; in fact, so much so it could be a little unsettling. Your characters are so similar in so many ways in that you are both optimistic, love to travel and generally have investigative and research-orientated personalities. Your discussions will be quite inspiring.

If Sagittarius joins with Leos born between 15 and 23 August a fantastic love affair is likely to ensue. Due to the rulership of Aries and Mars over them this will keep the passion and sexual exploration alive in your relationship for a long time. Both of you have a strong vitality and just as well because it looks like your physical relationship will require a little extra fuel, indeed.

SAGITTARIUS + VIRGO
Fire + Earth = Lava

You'll quickly learn that Virgo is concerned with minute matters, details and the fiddly aspects of life, which is very much in contrast to you, who can see the forest rather than the trees.

Virgo is under the rulership of Mercury, the planet of communication and speed. Virgo will be a challenge for you because of this very exacting attitude of theirs. It's not that you don't like to see things done properly but, to your way of thinking, Virgo is far too preoccupied with perfection. These differences in your personalities will not reconcile easily, that's for sure.

You must learn to accept that your views of the world and the way to do things are just so different and because Virgo seems such a critical star sign, you may be the one who will have to adjust yourself to their anxiousness about the many details of life. Putting all that aside, however, you will find that Virgo, being as intellectual as they are, will stimulate your own mental faculties. This is one aspect of the

Sagittarius–Virgo relationship that can work to your distinct advantage.

Virgo is the sign of the virgin and this doesn't mean that sex is abhorrent or out of the question, just that there's a certain innocence about how Virgo prefers to engage in the more intimate aspects of love. In this area as well you may need to work harder to develop harmony in your romance.

Astrologically speaking, you don't have a great deal of magnetic attraction to Virgos born between 24 August and 2 September, but it could be that there is a professional link between the two of you. Your initial connection through work could lead to a greater interest in each other once you become friends. This will then set the stage for a more romantic involvement.

Virgos born between 3 and 12 September will be hard work for you. They are not as active as you would like them and are probably more intellectually orientated. However, they will help you focus your energy practically and can even assist you in achieving your long-term objectives so there may be some merit to a relationship with these individuals.

The group of Virgos born between 13 and 23 September can get on your nerves so it's probably best to play the waiting game with them before becoming too involved. You need time to figure out how their minds work. You have great dissimilarities in the way you live your everyday lives so that may be too much of a challenge for you.

However, a good word for Virgo is that they will want to help you in any way they can.

SAGITTARIUS + LIBRA
Fire + Air = Hot air

This again is a great relationship based primarily on the compatibility of the elements that rule you both. You, Sagittarius, having fire as your element, and Libra being an air sign, indicates that the flames of your Sagittarian fire will burn brightly in the company of your Libran counterpart. Your warmth will also uplift and generate a great deal of inspiration for your Libran partner.

This is a relationship that can exhibit all the best traits of a relationship, including friendship, romance and good financial understanding as well. Librans make great friends to Sagittarius and support them in all of their endeavours. They can bring out the better qualities of your character as well.

Sagittarius and Libra do tend to have similarities, especially in their social activities. Like you, Libra enjoys the excitement offered by being with friends, studying humans and the world around them, and generally being out and about to absorb as much life and experiences as they can. Sounds much like you, doesn't it?

Taking long walks together either locally or through distant areas gives you the chance to get to know each other better. Your talks will be long and stimulating and this will help draw you closer.

Because you both have a love of travelling and gaining experiences from other cultures, there is every possibility you will meet each other while on vacation or travelling. There seems to be a lot of dynamics, activity and movement in your relationship.

Both of you will be continually on the go if you choose to spend your life together. There will never be a dull moment in this relationship.

Romance between a Sagittarius and Libran is always based on straightforward honesty and balance. You are open and share your deepest feelings with each other. This transparency is the stuff of which long-lasting relationships are made, and it is a great omen for success.

You'll feel relaxed together and the more you get to know each other the closer you will become. This includes your sexual compatibility as well.

Librans born between 24 September and 3 October can sometimes appear to be a little fickle and unstable to you, even though you like their independence. Finding satisfactory compromise in a romantic relationship with them might be a tricky affair.

Librans born between 4 and 13 October are exciting and like to do things in a progressive way. There is a touch of harmless craziness in them but this will spark your interest and give you many moments of pleasure and unexpected surprises as well.

There are great romantic opportunities and even marital prospects are likely with Librans born between 14 and 23 October. With Gemini and Mercury having an influence over them, and these astrological factors influencing your marriage strongly, it's likely this combination will be a no-brainer. Destiny with them is likely to be very powerful and rewarding.

SAGITTARIUS + SCORPIO
Fire + Water = Steam

If you think the sexual prowess of Scorpio has been a lot of hype, you'll soon learn this not at all true and, if you're after a deep, meaningful and sexual relationship, Scorpio is the sign to get involved with.

The big plus for the Sagittarius and Scorpio combination is the fact your ruling planets are quite friendly and therefore this is always a good foundation for a promising relationship together. The co-ruler of Scorpio, Mars, and your own ruler, Jupiter, when in concert produce big thinking and farsighted-ness so this will infuse your relationship with the same

41

qualities. Together your dreams will manifest and are likely to give you immense success together.

Your outgoing nature could be a bit too much for cautious Scorpio when you initially meet them, but they'll understand very quickly that you are genuine in your expression and this will go a long way towards winning their trust.

If you fall in love with a Scorpio the relationship will be extremely dynamic. A withdrawn Scorpio is not always as withdrawn as people imagine. Once they dedicate themselves to the partner of their choice, they open up and are even quite humorous in many respects, wanting to express their emotions with full intensity.

Scorpio has a tendency to hold grudges and they find it hard at times to let go of the past but with you by their side this could be much easier. Your social life and your love of the great outdoors will help distract them from these other negative emotions that tend to get the better of some of them.

Your love life together is extremely exciting and once you win the trust and support of a Scorpio they will admire your frank and open personality and even in some ways will try to emulate that. More than anything Scorpio wants to express how they feel, but with Pluto also ruling them, the hidden side of their nature often dominates their character. Slowly but surely, contact with your Sagittarian warmth will melt the icy waters of the Scorpio element.

Scorpios born between 24 October and 2 November are great partners for Sagittarius, especially those of you born between 2 and 11 December. This is a fiery and passionate combination and a good match for these star signs.

By far the best combination of Sagittarius and Scorpio is with those born between 3 and 12 November. With Jupiter and Neptune ruling them these individuals are not only creative and spiritual but also very compassionate and universal in their love. This can be a very successful union as well.

Love with a Scorpio born between 13 and 22 November brings a mixture of misunderstanding and confusion because of the influence of the Moon. You need to talk about your needs domestically and what you expect from family life so that you are both on the same page when it comes to these matters.

SAGITTARIUS + SAGITTARIUS
Fire + Fire = Explosion

This is an explosive combination that will either work or fail. Both of you are fire signs born under the same sign of Sagittarius and therefore you have similar thoughts and patterns of behaviour that need to be closely monitored if you want the relationship to work.

Your emotional energies are strong but you must both bring a measure of control over this aspect of your lives so you can propel the relationship forward rather than being bogged down in vying for dominance in the partnership.

Putting down your roots will also not be so easy because you have such an incredible love of freedom and independence at all costs. This is inherent in your nature. Freedom being the common thread means you can use it to forge a lifestyle unique to your own relationship; but if you pull in different directions, it is unlikely the relationship will survive.

'A rolling stone carries no moss', which could create a double problem for the dual-Sagittarian relationship. You are always on the go, setting your sights on the next objective, and therefore you might fail to secure a solid foundation. Balance your need for variety with a sense of security.

Honesty is the cornerstone of the relationship so this is the perfect element for ensuring you've both pulled together and appreciate each other. This relationship will naturally allow both of you to tear down the walls that obstruct who you are. It is a combination based on truth.

Loads of fun in your social life can be expected in this exciting match because you both make friends wherever you go.

Competitiveness is also an element of the Sagittarian personality so you'll find yourself trying to outdo each other but hopefully this will all be done with a sense of fun and fair play. You get on quite well with most Sagittarians but the class born between 23 November and 1 December are probably better suited to Sagittarians born on other dates. They have a great love of variety in love and social life and this will offer you a mutually supportive relationship and one in which your love will naturally flow.

I see a lot of travel together and visits to friends on a regular basis so you can expect plenty of fun times if your Sagittarian energy joins forces with theirs.

If you are with a Sagittarian born inside the 2 to 11 December period, Mars powerfully influences them so their physical appetites are particularly strong. You'll feel comfortable with them sexually and will also discover they have a strong need for doing sports and outdoor activities, which will be a bonus for your own health because they love their partners to be part of their exercise regime!

Sagittarians born between 12 and 22 December have strong solar and Leo energies marking their personality. You are attracted to their bright aura but they may want to control and change you. Once you've developed an additional dose of humility this relationship might have a good chance of working.

SAGITTARIUS + CAPRICORN

Fire + Earth = Lava

Your outgoing nature is vastly different from the Capricorn character. You have an open and straightforward approach and a very bright aura. Your easygoing approach to life tends to make you take things as they come. Somehow you always believe that life is going to work out for the best and, even if you are in a difficult situation, you trust you will land on your own two feet. This is the inner conviction that has brought you success and will continue to do so in the future.

Being quite the opposite to you, however, Capricorn doesn't necessarily believe this. Their motto is, 'Hope for the best, but expect the worst'. Due to the rulership of Saturn, the sombre and sometimes morose planet, they have a far more conservative and dull view of life. They are not anywhere near as optimistic as you are, Sagittarius.

It seems your primary role together will be Sagittarius's expectations to raise the optimism of Capricorn, while theirs will be to level yours and make you look at life from a more realistic perspective. This is not a bad thing for either of you, but if neither is prepared to budge from your viewpoint, there seems little reason for staying together in a relationship like this.

You have an adventurous and freedom-loving streak, which can spark the Capricornian sobriety. Although they are not generally drawn into these sorts of outdoor, high-level and competitive activities, some continued, gentle nudging might help them come out of their shell.

Capricorn is receptive, but slowly so. Your sexual chemistry with them might not be as hot and passionate as you'd like in the first instance; but then again, persistence usually pays off with Sagittarius.

Capricorn is actually considerably warmer and more loving than people give them credit for and your persistence will also discover this about Capricorn as well.

Teaming up with a Capricorn born between 23 December and 1 January is not likely to result in too passionate a relationship. These are down-to-earth types and need a lot of time and persuasion to bring them around to your warmth and passion.

Capricorns born between 1 and 10 January are emotional and sensual characters but you need to dig beneath the surface to bring that out of them. There's a certain attractiveness about these people that you are drawn to.

With Capricorns born between 11 and 20 January you can expect a wonderfully stimulating and enjoyable time. Believe it or not these individuals are quite humorous in nature but I must warn you now that Capricorn is somewhat dry and cynical. Keep an open mind and you could have lots of fun times with them.

SAGITTARIUS + AQUARIUS
Fire + Air = Hot air

The hot flaming fires of Sagittarius work well with the Aquarian element of air so I can assure you that this combination is a positive omen for a relationship. Both of you are always busy and active, always on the go, extending yourself in both your personal and professional lives. Together you will feel synergistically connected and will enjoy a bustling social scenario with each other.

You're intrigued by the progressive attitude of Aquarius and the fact that they like to be constantly engaged with social and communal activities. Apart from the usual theatrical or club scene, Aquarius is genuinely interested in helping the world and doing something worthwhile. Because of your own leanings towards spirituality, these concepts appeal to you. You could find common ground in these areas.

On occasion Aquarians tend to go through the most incredibly unexpected shifts and changes in their lives. If you are involved in a relationship with them you might find it hard to understand how such radical changes seem to happen to them. At the drop of a hat they'll up and leave without a moment's notice. This could leave you high and dry, if not broken hearted, so you should always learn a little more about Aquarius before committing your heart too soon.

Actually, you might quickly find that the Aquarian partner you are with is quite rebellious by nature and doesn't like to be stifled in any shape or form. In fact, they take a certain pleasure in bucking authority and want to live life on their own terms, irrespective of what other people think. You too like freedom but the Aquarian brand of freedom is unique and could even rattle your Sagittarian sensibilities from time to time.

The sexual aspect of your relationship is dramatic and at times tense, but nevertheless exciting and passionate due to the electric energies of the planet Uranus, which rules Aquarius. A great deal of vibrant energy will come your way if you find yourself sexually involved with an Aquarian. You are both exploratory when it comes to matters of intimacy so this will be a constantly evolving relationship in the bedroom, much to both of your satisfaction.

By becoming involved with Aquarians born between 21 and 30 January you'll be quite surprised to find just how strong willed they are. A clash of minds is likely with them so you need to take extra precautions if you are serious about a relationship. Actually, all you need with this group of Aquarians is a great deal of mental flexibility

Aquarians born between 31 January and 8 February have Mercury and Gemini strongly influencing them. Because of this, marriage and a lifelong friendship is likely to result in your association with them. These people can bring you great fulfilment.

With Aquarians born between 9 and 19 February you'll be drawn romantically to them, particularly if you're born between 23 November and 1 December. Romantic and lucky Venus will help them soothe your soul because it is also co-rules their birth. In their company you'll feel loved and cherished. This is a strong reciprocal love relationship for both of you.

SAGITTARIUS + PISCES
Fire + Water = Steam

The benevolent Jupiter is your ruler Sagittarius and coincidentally it also rules Pisces. Because of this the lucky vibrations of the planet extend to both of your lives and this is a particularly favourable omen because you have much in common and will be attracted romantically.

There's a natural and intuitive link between Sagittarius and Pisces. Both of you have a spiritual and sensitive element due to the vibrations of your common ruling planet, and Pisces will appreciate your compassionate and generous energies.

Pisces is incredibly psychic being the last of the zodiac signs and is sometimes considered the most evolved among us. Trying to withhold your feelings or secrets from Pisces doesn't work as they are able to intuit exactly what's on your mind.

You find Pisces quite attractive due to their idealism and you both agree that life is more than just what we experience with our senses. The philosophies work well together and this is extremely important for the success of any relationship.

As with most relationships, you also have some differences that need to be kept in mind. For starters, your fiery energy, Sagittarius, could be a little too intense for the receptive and easygoing Pisces. You live life at a much faster pace and this could cause them to either cringe or retaliate. Fire warms water but by the same tendency can also boil it. Remember that.

Pisces is the consummate dreamer. They live in a world of spiritual ideals, and need time for those dreams to manifest. You on the other hand are spontaneous and need instant gratification, preferring to live by your wits from moment to moment. These two diametrically opposed attitudes could erode the fabric of your partnership.

The domestic side of Pisces and their nurturing ways make them excellent family people. They feel creative as nurturers and carers and you'll never be in need of anything should you choose to spend the rest of your life with them. Trying to get them to think practically or in the way that the average person thinks is another matter, however, but you'll always be loved and supported by them in their own way.

The sexual and emotional aspirations of Sagittarius and Pisces are also similar so you could expect a very fulfilling physical interplay. Sexually speaking, you are both extremely compatible.

You have similar interests to Pisces born between 20 and 28 or 29 February. These people are very intuitive and possibly even clairvoyant so you should always listen to what their vibes tell them, as their hunches are usually correct.

Move slowly with Pisceans born between 1 and 10 March. They are such emotional beings whose sensitivity will be a little too much for you to deal with. They are particularly finicky about how you should save or spend your money.

Mixing with Pisceans born between 11 and 20 March will be a positive experience for you. Mars, Pluto and Jupiter influence their personalities. There are some secretive elements to this relationship so be prepared for a different type of love if you're serious about getting involved with them.

2009:
The Year Ahead

*We should all be concerned about the future because we will
have to spend the rest of our lives there.*

—Charles F. Kettering

Romance and friendship

Your Sagittarian need for adventure and exploration is fulfilled
this year due to the exciting placement of Venus as the year
commences. Being in your zone of travels and communication,
your personal style will be absolutely attractive to the other
sex. You can win over people by a gesture or a sweet word and
you can expect lots of travel and communication to be linked
to your romantic life, particularly in the first month of the year.

Seek balance so that you don't wear yourself out too early
in the year. You are so vital and energetic and want to lift your
current relationships to a new level of magic and inspiration.
But don't go overboard. Use a measure of caution in new relationships, which could be numerous. You'll have plenty of new
opportunities and friendships from which to choose so take
your time and above all carefully analyse those with whom you
come in contact. Don't assume that everyone is going to fulfil
your wildest dreams in 2009. There is a responsibility attached
to any new friendship you develop.

Your public image will be important to you throughout
January and February but you may not feel totally accepted for
who you are. This will bring its own set of challenges, which
you will have to deal with. In January you may have second
thoughts about a relationship you are in and this could also be
a reflection of these very same aspects of how you truly feel
about yourself. Developing self-confidence will be the key to
making your relationships work and creating a fulfilling atmos-
phere for your personal affairs.

After the 15th you will experience more excitement in your
life when Venus and Uranus combine. This could, however,
have an unsettling effect on your family affairs, especially if

others are out of step with what you believe is your right to explore new relationships. You could find yourself in a conflict of wills with other family members who disapprove of your choices. It may be a better idea to keep some of your newfound friends a secret until you gain a deeper understanding of their personalities and true motives.

In February Venus brings with it a dose of amorous energy and injects your life with new rays of hope for being in love. This is an exciting time; your previous self-doubts have eased and you have a great deal of confidence dealing with others. During this period you'll find your standards and moral views shifting somewhat due to a very important lunar eclipse occurring in your zone of philosophy, religion and higher ideals.

This could be an important transition from your past ways to a future potential. Around the 12th, however, you could feel confused as these matters are never easy to resolve, especially in the context of society and conventional attitudes. You will probably continue to work through these problems for some time to come, particularly with electric Uranus continuing its trek through your zone of domestic harmony.

In the latter part of February family members will place additional demands on you that will take you away from the limelight of love and social life. Settling down and executing some of the more unsavoury responsibilities will be part of this cycle. Fortunately the planets Mars and the Sun are relatively quick moving and not long lasting in effect (but usually intense). Keep your wits about you and try not to get embroiled in head-on confrontations when people challenge your views.

Your love life will intensify in March, especially when Venus moves into reverse motion. You may realise that there have been aspects of your partner's personality you've overlooked or turned a blind eye to, even though you may have been fully aware of the consequences of being with someone who thinks and behaves the way they do. Up until the middle of April you may have to reconsider your strategies in dealing with these parts of your partner's character. This is a learning curve for you and if handled correctly you'll come out a winner in a much more fulfilling relationship as a whole.

At this time your creative powers are strong as well. Some women who are of child-bearing age may put a lot of energy into this part of their lives. Issues of motherhood, family life and pregnancy could become very important items on your agenda. If you're married and feeling financially secure, it could be the perfect time to consider mother or fatherhood.

For those of you who are still playing the field, however, this continues to be an excellent time to extend your social circle, meet new people and generally enjoy going out, partying and understanding more about the world and your place in it.

If you have an artistic streak, your creative abilities will improve at this time and you'll find more meaning within yourself and in how you express this creative talent through your chosen hobby or activity. You may discover something new about yourself that will further enamour others. You'll become attractive, charming and will not have too much of a problem making friends.

Throughout April and May your sexual influence is strong and you will need to find an adequate outlet for these energies. Mars and Venus in conjunction are notorious for their persuasive power in the bedroom. Hopefully you have someone to share these exciting energies with otherwise you may become frustrated, especially if you don't have an adequate outlet. Generally, however, this time should be less stressful and physically vital.

Any misunderstandings in your friendships will be cleared up after the 18th of April. You must listen to the other person's point of view. Your ruling planet Jupiter will be in a tricky position causing your ego to be inflated. Even if you are correct on a technical point, you may have to concede for the sake of keeping the peace.

Mercury enters your zone of public relations after the 2nd of May and this is a great period for dealing with the world. Your communication will be strong and you'll be curious about learning more about the nature of relationships and how to improve your social skills. You could, however, be a little too enthusiastic and may even alienate friends by trying to shove your opinions down their throat. Keep a balance between speaking and listening.

If you're a hard worker, business could take precedence over your love life throughout June and July. In fact, you could become a workaholic and ignore the needs of your partner through your one-eyed attitude. If you're married or in a long-term committed relationship, you may feel that your hard work is creating a more secure future for your family, but you could be oblivious of your family's emotional requirements.

Marriage, engagements and other traditional love cere-monies are likely to surface after the 5th of July. This could even be your own matrimonial announcement! On the other hand, you may hear news of someone else's love, engagement or marriage and will be the recipient of an invitation to attend a friend's or relative's celebrations. It is likely that you will be playing a part in one of these celebrations throughout this cycle.

Sex and money are tied in the next month. If the sizzle has gone out of your love life, August is a time when you may invest money in accessories that can enhance your mood such as sexy lingerie, scented candles, incense and other mood enhancing objects. This will definitely lift your lovemaking to a new level.

Under the auspicious influence of Venus in your zone of travels in September, you have the opportunity to start planning a journey connected with some social engagement. You may have to postpone this for a while, however. You will connect will friends or school mates at some sort of reunion at this time.

October may not be the easiest of times. Communicating your feelings or drawing out your partner's feelings may be a difficult task. A cooling off of your emotions is likely but an understanding and sympathetic approach to communicating your dissatisfaction will foster a deeper tie with your loved one.

The last part of the year is exciting with Venus triggering your social appetites. November will be a bustling time up until the 8th, after which you may need time to recuperate. Too much of a good thing will create the reverse effect. You'll feel lighter in spirit after the previous difficulty with loved ones. Your romantic and social lives enter a new phase.

The last month is an excellent moment for the closure of 2009. Looking and feeling your best seems to be the theme for December. Your sense of self is strong and your ties of friendship solidify. Venus and Mars also enter a friendly phase, ushering in opportunities to formalise your partnerships and romance, especially if you have been undecided about whether or not to take it further. You can do so now with confidence.

Work and money

With Saturn continuing its influence on your professional activities throughout 2009, you must expect your responsibilities to remain with you just a little longer. This will change later in the year and you will have a wonderful sense of relief by hanging in there and doing your work to the best of your ability.

Most of your planets occupy the finance zone of your horoscope as this year commences showing just how committed and focused you are on getting ahead financially. You'll be making some significant changes to the way you handle money in 2009. There is a tremendous emphasis on doing your best to earn money that points at new ways of increasing your cash flow.

You'll hardly be back at work in January before your new attitude and philosophy over work and money will begin to be implemented. You must take some precautions in sharing your ideas or discussing financial issues with your family members and business partners because you're likely to be rather head-strong and particularly inflexible in your opinions. This could, in the early part of the year, cause a few problems for you. After the 12th of January when Mercury goes retrograde, you'll have insufficient information to make important decisions, so it's best to hold off until you are in possession of all the facts you need.

Venus and Pluto cause you to make radical changes in your financial planning in February. You must be prepared to be more flexible to adjust to situations that are going to make your financial position a lot healthier. There may even be important decisions surrounding your profession. This may not be too easy, especially if you have become accustomed to the type of work and routine of your particular vocation. New contractual arrangements after the 15th are great and open new doors for you.

Your career planet Mercury is activated in the early part of March and you'll be busy planning and implementing your plans throughout this month and April. Excellent transits to your professional sign after the 6th of April ensure some great deals due to your communication ability. The Sun also sets in motion new developments in your work after the 20th and you are likely to feel rather proud of yourself. With Mars moving to your creative zone as well, you can feel confident that your work performance will be recognised. You should feel on top of things.

June will be testy for you, especially if you're working at close quarters with others who are just as ambitious as you. Co-workers could be cantankerous or demanding and, if you are in a subordinate position with a boss who is overly demanding, it could be very trying, indeed. This will cause you to become restless and to imagine other professional possibilities. Sometimes a difficult situation can ultimately lead to a better career situation in the end, so keep your options open and don't be afraid to investigate alternatives. June will be a good time to do this.

June can be also a little hectic generally and this will be the case when the Sun enters your eighth zone of tax and shared resources after the 21st. You need to keep a cool head, especially if your taxation or financial adviser is telling you things you don't believe. The responsibility is yours to question and make the appropriate changes to your financial planning if you feel this is necessary. You may have some disagreements with those who are serving you. In the interests of your own future financial security, you're the one who has to make the final decision. Be bold and take control of your money and your career.

Fine negotiations can be expected throughout July, with Mercury and Saturn indicating you are able to focus your attention clearly on your work and career objectives. If you have clients or others you deal with on a regular basis, they will be more than happy to provide you with extra business. This should result in a surplus of cash and sales.

In September and October Venus brings interesting social opportunities through your working associations. It will be a happy time of the year when you feel comfortable with your work and social life. They will work well together and your personality flows in such a way that others help you achieve your goals. You can also put these talents to use in approaching other companies for a new job with a more lucrative position if you choose.

I mentioned earlier that Saturn was causing you some problems and perhaps a greater sense of responsibility throughout its transit but, after the 30th of October when it moves to your zone of profits and general life fulfilment, you'll feel a lessening of the load in your professional area. Actually, Saturn and the eleventh zone together are considered an excellent omen in astrology.

The remainder of the year should see a general improvement and specifically an upliftment in your professional status if you're prepared to take a few gambles.

Karma, luck and meditation

Your lucky planets are Jupiter, Mars and the Sun. The Sun in particular is your planet of past karma and indicates the benefits you can expect through past good deeds.

An excellent forecast occurs in 2009 due to the fact that these three significant planets are conjoined as the year commences, and in your finance zone at that. This will definitely be a lucky year for you and in particular most Sagittarians can expect their bank balance to increase.

While money does seem to be an area of good luck for you, we mustn't forget the natural ruler of karma, which is Saturn, and that it is still currently passing through your zone of professional activities, the highest point in your horoscope. So, this year you will still be burdened with additional work issues that need to be sorted out. Fortunately by October the fog will lift and you'll be able to enjoy fully the benefits of your hard work.

The last week of February is fortunate when Jupiter makes a wonderful aspect to your Sun sign, creating a great deal of optimism and opportunities with people with whom you are in contact. Gifts, favours and other gestures of goodwill can be anticipated throughout February and March.

In April the Sun creates some nice opportunities for you and communications will be high on your agenda, particularly between the 2nd and the 11th. The ideas you share with others will be the basis for some new prospects that can be converted into cash.

A lucky month for romance is July in which marital–engagement opportunities present themselves. There is also a repeat of this around September when Venus enters your lucky ninth zone. You should feel happy in your current relationships or, if you're on the lookout for a soulmate, this is the time when magic can and will happen. Some of your wildest dreams could come true!

SAGITTARIUS

2009:
Month by Month
Predictions

The past can't see you, but the future is listening.

—Destin Figuier

Highlights of the month

You are preoccupied with financial matters and, from the 2nd when Mercury enters your finance zone, new business or financial opportunities bring a smile to your face. Communications regarding these matters are also highlighted at this time but around the 4th you'll also have the chance to spend some quality time at home and share some of these exciting opportunities with your loved ones.

An important transition takes place around the 6th of January when your ruling planet enters the third zone of communication, travels, education and daily activities. This is a new cycle that lasts for approximately one year. You'll be spending time in this arena of your life, perhaps investigating new educational or travel opportunities and, along with the great professional monetary opportunities that present themselves, this period will prove to be a very exciting time, indeed.

The issue of legal matters is not one that will affect all Sagittarians but for those who have been waiting on a verdict for some work compensation claim, outstanding will or legacy, the combination of the Sun and Mercury after the 21st is an excellent time to receive news that will boost your assurance that these matters are now coming to a close. The presence of Jupiter is also superb for any contractual arrangements you may be contemplating. Due to the retrogression of Mercury, however, it is probably best to wait a few weeks before firmly making a decision and signing on the dotted line.

Sudden events are not necessarily disruptive but could spin your head around between the 23rd and the 25th. A decision made or an assurance given by someone might test your level of faith and confidence in them. Actually, this is all probably a storm in a teacup so don't let the situation get the better of you and try to use humour to get through what will at first seem a dicey situation.

An important solar eclipse takes place on the 26th and may affect the relationship you have with neighbours, close friends or even a younger brother or sister. If you're trying to help someone at this time could be well worth mentioning the fact that handing over bad money after good is not necessarily the proper course of action to achieve the result you want. Helping others to help themselves would be more appropriate at this time if you feel as if you're beating your head against the wall. Remain relaxed!

An excellent romantic combination takes place in the heavens around the 27th. You'll be feeling happy in your friendships and discussions you have with someone at this time could make you feel very special.

With Mercury joining Mars on the 28th, try to be more lenient in your approach to money and the way others in the family wish to spend or save. You may find that you have a difference of opinion over these issues. Live and let live.

Romance and friendship

You have a passionate streak in you on the 5th and need to prove that your seductive and charming ways can attract others. You'll have ample opportunity to show what you're made of; however, this could also attract the displeasure of a friend or two, especially if they have their eyes set on the same person. You mustn't let love become a wedge between you and good friends. Talk about your feelings openly before going in for 'the kill'.

On the 8th your sense of humour may well be appreciated by people of your own age but if you happen to be in the company of those who are a little more stodgy and old-fashioned than your usual group of acquaintances, you might raise a few eyebrows. Be mindful of the circumstances you find yourself in before opening your mouth and putting your foot in it. You can impress others with your quick wit and humorous stories between the 8th and 12th.

On the 15th you are still all systems go and will find it hard to slow down during this current planetary period. It's a good idea to let off steam through exercise and as much physical activity as possible. It would be a shame to find yourself stuck behind a desk, bored out of your mind with only mental activities as company, when the big, wide world is calling you. It's a good time to travel rather than postponing it to a later date. The spirit of adventure is also very strong in you on the 18th.

Between the 26th and 28th it's a good time for you to shine and show the world just what you're made of. Your popularity will be notable now and there are many opportunities to meet new people who will give you a different spin on life. You'll have a tendency to gamble or at least take some chance on love.

Work and money

Between the 6th and 8th you could regret impromptu gestures of generosity, especially if you're giving away money or things to someone you scarcely know. It's best to appraise the credentials of anyone you meet and above all don't try to impress others with your open-handedness. You will need some extra cash and will kick yourself later on if you find yourself short of a dollar or two.

Your moods can quickly change from one of pleasure seeking to serious business acumen on the 14th. It will be like day turning into night but this is good because you will realise it is the time to get back to the grindstone to forge some new successes in the coming months. You generally have the support of most of those you work with but do be careful as there may well be a rival lurking in the shadows—someone whom you least expect it to be, too!

You will have to dedicate much more time to a particular activity around the 29th if you want to become great at it. Success is not something that accidentally falls in your lap. It requires a lot of hard work and you realise this.

Positive: 2, 4, 15, 21

Negative: 14

Mixed: 5, 6, 7, 8, 9, 10, 11, 12, 23, 24, 25, 26, 27, 28, 29

Highlights of the month

This is one of the better times of the year to pursue your romantic dreams and, with Venus spicing up your love life after the 3rd and Mars also casting at a glance in your direction, you'll hyped up to take advantage of any and every social engagement that is presented. You will also make quite an impression wherever you go.

There may be moments where you could be caught off guard with impromptu offers or invitations, so don't forget to take or keep an extra garment in the car so you can make a quick change to look your best for what could be the odd glamorous occasion. On the 5th, 6th, 9th and 10th, relations could be a little strained but this won't hold you back from enjoying February to the max.

A lunar eclipse in Leo on the 10th reveals something of your past to you which can either be seen in a positive or negative light, depending on your frame of mind. Even if what you discover is a little unsavoury, this is still an opportunity for you to improve yourself and to use this as 'fertiliser' for spiritual growth.

Because the Sun creates a rather difficult aspect around the 11th, your pride or ego may be wounded by learning the truth about how someone feels about you. This again is a prime opportunity for you to strengthen the inner core of your being and my suggestion is to not let these things get the better of you. People may say or do things but this shouldn't be taken to heart. Remember the old saying, 'Sticks and stones …'?

Lucky opportunities, gifts and other favourable connections can be expected between the 18th and the 20th when Venus, Mars and the Sun all provide you with beneficial rays of hope and a little glory thrown in for good measure. This is likely to be an excellent period in your work and any assistance you require will be easily provided to you. You'll also want to spend a little more time on the home front, however, so balancing both of these areas of your life could be a challenge this month.

Your immense drive and determination is visible after the 21st when Mars injects your Sun sign with copious amounts of physical energy. You're unstoppable at this time but may also steamroll a few people whose only intention is to help you. Try to remain sensitive as you could end up having to do more work on your own when a few extra pairs of hands were available after all. Listen to the advice others have to give you.

Romance and friendship

Love is definitely in the air and you'll want something out of the ordinary between the 1st and 6th. By all means explore all possibilities but don't wear your heart on your sleeve.

You will be torn between your social obligations and setting aside enough time and energy for a passion or hobby between the 7th and the 10th. It's simply a matter of prioritising your activities and, if you happen to alienate someone by not giving them enough time, this may have to be the price you pay for a future success.

On the 15th you're probably run down from too much partying, which is why you need some time to recharge your batteries. It's not a bad idea also to get in touch with who you are and work out what you really want throughout 2009 and beyond.

On the 17th and 18th you continue to have the beneficial influence of Venus on your closest romantic and marital relationships. You should use this to maximum benefit and if there is something you would like from your lover, now is the time to ask for it. There's hardly any chance at all that they will refuse you. Use your luck wisely.

Between the 25th and 28th your philosophical views may be at odds with your partner, especially if you have been developing your spiritual interests. You will be so enthusiastic that you come across as a crusader trying to convert the other person to your way of thinking. It's best to ask questions rather than make statements. This way you least appear to be interested in the other person's opinion and will have a better chance of convincing them of your perspective as well.

Work and money

It seems as if your long-term personal and financial objectives can be fairly well worked out to your satisfaction after the 4th. You'll be feeling good about yourself so enjoy the blessings of the planets.

Between the 18th and 23rd your financial karma is strong and positive as the opportunity to earn a good deal of money seems promising. Of course, if you've been stuck in a rut, a job you know all too well, making the break could be harder than you think even though the proverbial bag of gold is visible at the end of the rainbow. The chance to gain success is as dependent on your courage and earnestness as much as anything else.

On the 18th, one good deed deserves another. Repaying a debt or favour may be hanging over your head but you possibly don't have time to make good on the promise of squaring off this debt. The longer you leave it the guiltier you'll feel and, of course, the respect you would like to receive from others could diminish as a result. It's best to get this out of the way and repay what's outstanding.

A serious bent of mind is necessary to complete the task between the 22nd and 28th, even though others would have you make light of the situation. Keep your level of concentration consistent and don't digress from the task you have set yourself. Financial issues will also bother you but with your keen focus you can break the back of this problem as well. Banking matters will appear complex but can be simple things to clear so don't stress about them.

Positive: 1, 2, 3, 4, 17, 18, 19, 20, 21

Negative: 11, 15

Mixed: 5, 6, 9, 10, 22, 23, 24, 25, 26, 27, 28

Highlights of the month

Although your career ruler Mercury is at the bottom end of your horoscope it will stimulate you to think carefully about your professional prospects, albeit in a more private and cloistered environment. In fact, some Sagittarians may choose to do more work from home this month as Mercury moves through the domestic zone of their horoscope.

Between the 6th and the 8th the opportunity to share love and friendship is strong. I see many mutual benefits to your relationships and partly this has to do with your openness and the generosity of friends that you surround yourself with during this period.

It is likely you will also develop a more compassionate streak in your nature and, if you find yourself a little too self-absorbed and attentive to your own needs, that will quickly turn around this month when you choose to help someone with their problems and cast aside your own concerns for just a little while. You will find yourself concerned about reconnecting with those with whom you've neglected or not been able to spend enough time. This is a time when you should take a few steps towards friends to prove the calibre of your own love and friendship. Goodwill is one of your main key words this month.

If you happen to be feeling frustrated after the 11th, the easiest solution is to get mobile and try not to get bogged down with the situation or the people in it. Saturn will still be pushing you to your limits and testing you as far as co-workers and employers are concerned.

A powerful sense of responsibility is likely to weigh upon your shoulders and you might feel as if you've been landed with an unfair amount of the workload. Take a mini break during this period because it could serve you well and will certainly defuse the situation with your co-workers. Relationships with authoritarian figures and in particular men yielding a big stick could be a problem for you.

There may be other areas that need to be addressed at this time, especially if you're feeling a little out of sync with any fad, fashion or general consensus. You'll be firmly entrenched in your own opinions. However, after the 24th you may be opposed by someone whose perspectives and feelings are just as strong as yours but not necessarily in agreement. An element of compromise will be most important to keep the peace. Try not to force the issue because it will only back fire.

This month is particularly favourable for bringing the family together and holding a function or party in your home. Long-lost relatives and other friends who have been out of the loop should all be brought together to celebrate life, simply for the sake of enjoying each other's company. You don't necessarily need any particular reason this month except to revel in the joy of being with loved ones. The period of the 25th to the 27th is excellent for these sorts of activities.

Romance and friendship

To improve the quality of your relationships between the 1st and 5th you both need to be physically active and connected through movement or exercise. This will lift your emotional state to a new high and give you a sense of confidence that your relationship can indeed deepen even further. This is a time of bonding with your loved ones.

Although you wish to be part of the social scene on the 12th, you could be mentally a little lazy and you're not at all into making the effort to understand anything new. This could cause a problem if others are expecting you to be the life of the party. You will need to find a quiet corner at the next gathering and camouflage yourself as a pot plant, particularly after the 16th.

You mustn't let pride get in the road of developing a friendship with someone you've just met on the 19th. Your initial reaction will give way to a feeling of closeness and deep interest in this new character. While you shouldn't be too effusive or impulsive, you mustn't by the same token turn away from any fresh romantic opportunity.

You need to look at unconventional ways of developing your inner wisdom and spiritual growth between the 24th and 28th. If your methods have been habitual and the people you have associated with in this respect have also been 'old hat', this is the time for revolution and a new way.

A friend could be a stick in the mud around the 30th and you will feel obliged to play the victim by making them feel better. The fact of the matter is you don't really need this person (or anyone else) to drag you down, especially when what you want is fun and relaxation. You need to read them the Riot Act.

Work and money

Between the 1st and 9th you enter a new cycle in which your efforts are supported by a quietly confident and relaxed optimism that what you need will turn up at the appropriate time without too much effort on your part. You'll be surprised at the success you generate with this very unique attitude. The universe will indeed shortly provide you with some interesting professional surprises.

If you happen to have overspent you might be regretting your extravagances when you are unable to join in with work colleagues at an event on the 11th. You need to count the pennies so that you are available to enjoy some of the extra social activities that are likely to be presented to you. Apart from the social enjoyment, you want to be available for any career-networking opportunities as well.

A new real estate deal or a change of residence is likely for some Sagittarians between the 22nd and 25th. This cycle indicates that your desire for change on the home front will be forthcoming as well as justified. As they say, a change is as good as a holiday, and this may be sufficient to rejuvenate you for what's ahead.

Positive: 1, 2, 3, 4, 5, 6, 7, 8, 22, 23, 25, 26, 27, 28

Negative: 12, 30

Mixed: 11, 19, 24

Highlights of the month

Keep your wits about you in the early part of this month because you are likely to be forgetful or probably distracted by your own thoughts. This is not to say you don't have a wealth of ideas and between the 1st and the 3rd you come up with moments of genius where your work or future prospects are concerned. A problem occurs after the 5th, however, when Mars and Saturn enter into a difficult transition.

You may feel extremely frustrated and even abstracted by someone in your immediate environment. If your ideas are sensible—even though in some ways a little too highbrow—there may be no logical reason why anyone should oppose your way of thinking. But this is exactly what may happen. You could feel unsupported, unloved, or downright solitary for a while and may need to rely wholly and solely on your own inner resources.

You will regain some of your inner confidence and peace of mind by the 11th but, irrespective of what you do in the first part of April, you may not be able please everyone all the time. At some point you'll rub someone in the wrong way and regret having done it. Try to accept that this is not the easiest of months, that the planets continue their motion into different cycles and any difficulties can and do pass in due course.

Mercury enters your zone of work activities, daily planning and employment. A great way to get rid of some of your tension, especially after the 14th, is to direct your energy into your work practices and improve your skills in this area. The Sun and Mars give you a whole new spin on life and you'll find your ingenuity at an all-time high. Venus may also cause you a few problems with friends and those closest to you, but they will accommodate your needs and bring you some much-desired affection if you approach them in a different way, on their terms.

Your thinking is clear and precise between the 18th and 22nd. At this time you can now make some headway with those sceptics or other cynics who may not have believed in you. This is your chance to prove your worth, to step up to the plate to take your ideas to the world in a big way. Now, if you happen to be a homemaker who doesn't deal at the boardroom level, don't think that these planetary influences won't affect you. You have just as much opportunity for hatching an idea and proving your abilities in your own domestic circle of influence. Don't give up and keep trying until you reach your goal. The planets are behind you during this phase.

After the 24th you can continue organising your life in such a way that befits your vision of a wonderful future. This is a fact-finding week so do everything you can to put all the pieces of the jigsaw in place to your own satisfaction, irrespective of what others have to say about your doing it.

Romance and friendship

You will meet someone who acts as a mentor who can show you the way between the 1st and 5th. Their friendship will not only inspire you but will give you moments of laughter.

You can be a daredevil between the 5th and 8th and attempt something you haven't tried before—even what you once thought might have been impossible—if you wish. In any case, you want a distinct break with your usual routine and by doing so will make this jovial time just that little bit more exciting and memorable. Believe it or not, a friend of yours is also in the same frame of mind as you so they will be prepared to share this excitement with you.

You have to balance obligation against your need to break free of hindering individuals. Between the 13th and 15th someone who has been a weight on your shoulders for some time will be ready for you to cut them free. This doesn't mean you won't continue to be friends but it does indicate an important turning point for them in which they will have to take responsibility for their own actions and problems. You're free at last!

Between the 23rd and 25th you can let your guard down and use a little humour to get you across the line without too many worries. Feeling relaxed and confident, you're ready to expand your social circle and learn many new things about yourself and others. It's an exciting month so don't say no to any offers of love or friendship. Some significant lessons will be learned by you between the 26th and 30th. It's a time of incredible growth.

You will have serious issues associated with commitment—either your own or someone else's—around the 12th. If you've been waiting around for someone to put the ring on your finger then you may be hanging around quite a bit longer. You will just have to put your foot down if settling down is what you want.

Work and money

The Sun and Jupiter make you a little more wasteful but this won't worry you around the 11th because you feel that fun and pleasure should take precedence over financial prudence. Ethical and moral issues also take centre stage as you are confronted by someone and a situation that challenges the very core of your work beliefs.

You reach a new high in the cycle of your profession or studies between the 18th and 23rd and you're likely to find yourself the recipient of some good luck or even a gift from someone you least expect. This will occur after the new moon of the 25th, which is also an excellent time to rekindle projects that have been on the backburner for a while.

A choice between two lines of work or study could be difficult after the 26th because both have equally promising prospects in the future. This is a matter of research and careful analysis on your part, but don't miss a key clue around the 28th that will set the trend for the rest of the month and perhaps your future in general as well. You'll be feeling pretty good about your health and vitality at this time.

Positive: 1, 2, 3, 4, 6, 7, 8, 11, 13, 14, 15, 17, 18, 19, 20, 21, 22, 23, 24, 25

Negative: 12, 26

Mixed: 5

Highlights of the month

Your heightened popularity is a result of your excellent public-relations skills this month, due to the favourable placement of Mercury. You have drive, energy and, as well, your suave and convincing words will make achieving your goals that much easier.

Between the 2nd and the 7th you should move quickly to secure agreements and contracts because Mercury again moves retrograde. If after this you are lacking in the information you need to make a balanced decision, back off.

Your lucky planet, the Sun, causes you to work a little bit harder than you should. You need to rely on the luck factor rather than feeling as if you have to exert too much effort this month. Tidying up unfinished business at your workplace and also removing the backlog will be paramount in giving you a more peaceful mind. In the earlier part of the month you should avoid this workaholic drive and create some worthwhile social time after the 17th.

Between the 18th and the 21st, partnerships thrive. There's no holding you back from gaining what you want in your relationships. There won't be too much of a need to convince your spouse or partner of what you desire because they will be amenable to making it happen for you.

During this same period, listen carefully to what is said as the hard aspect of Mercury and Jupiter could cause you to misinterpret some directions or important information, particularly if the discussions happen to be by telephone. If you do miss a pertinent piece of data you could spend an awful lot of time back-pedalling later, trying to sort out the issue.

If you've had difficulty bridging your vision of life with the practical reality of where you happen to be, you'll be pleased to note that some time after the 27th the pieces fall together as if by magic. Your luck factor is strong with Mars and Jupiter favourably influencing you and Neptune also giving you the opportunity to make concrete those dreams you thought may only ever remain dreams. Use the power, privilege and contacts of your social and family circles to better your prospects in life generally.

From the 29th to the 31st you'll become pretty inventive and will want to share and manifest your concepts with those who can make a difference in your life. Your originality is what is going to count just now and this applies to the most simple and mundane tasks of your life as well.

Romance and friendship

Have you been drinking a little too heavily or eating too many sweets? Between the 3rd and the 7th could be the perfect time to recommit to your previous new year's resolution and cut back on those calories. As well as looking much better, you'll inject yourself with a dose of health and vitality.

Between the 17th and 22nd it's a time of high living and socialising for you, so enjoy yourself as much as possible! Several romantic opportunities are likely to present themselves and, would you believe, you may choose to investigate all of them, not just one! This is not a bad idea at all if you want to play the comparison game and choose the pick of the crop.

Prepare yourself for a change of scene and a new batch of people who will stimulate your mind and your body as well after the 27th. If you've been bored with your usual circle of friends, it is likely that this won't last long. The coming days will offer you plenty of variety and romantic escapades. If you are currently in a relationship, this could see a revival of passion—much to your satisfaction.

You may have overdosed on family and relatives and might need to escape to some secluded corner of the house, if not another city. There are demands on you on the 30th, which are wearing a little thin. This is only because you haven't had the courage to draw the line and let others know what you will or won't do. If you're feeling stifled, you only have yourself to blame.

Work and money

If you've been far too disciplined in everything you're doing, this month is your chance to relax a little and enjoy the fruits of your labour. For some Sagittarians it will have seemed like hard work rather than pleasure. A friend will come to your rescue after the 5th and help you work out a problem.

Your finances could be in a ditch for a while and, even though you know you're the one to blame for this, remain positive because things improve by the 17th. If you're working in a part-time job that is not paying much, you'll be feeling emotional between the 18th and 21st and should surely try to make the break and attempt something new. Do so as long as it doesn't jeopardise your finances further, though.

You will not be in the mood for any sort of serious study and will throw all cares to the wind by the 26th. Don't fight this, particularly because you're not likely to get any real quality work done during this time frame anyway. Enjoy yourself and then get down to the nitty gritty of studious deadlines, particularly after the 29th. You will fare much better at this time.

Positive: 17, 26, 27, 29, 31

Negative: Nil

Mixed: 2, 3, 4, 5, 6, 7, 18, 19, 20, 21, 30

Highlights of the month

I strongly recommend you take care this month and look after your health better, sleep more and give yourself a good deal of time to get to your destination, especially if travelling by car. It is likely due to the presence of Mars in a critical area of your horoscope that mishaps, health issues and other problems may occur. Between the 1st and the 5th, if you happen to be working with machinery, electrical equipment and other devices, take extra care to read the instructions and not be impulsive or impatient. This way you can avoid unnecessary accidents or injuries.

Venus is lucky for you while it remains in your zone of love affairs. It promises an improvement in your social popularity and also a bigger dose of affection from the one you love if you are currently in a relationship. On the 3rd and 4th you could be showered with love and gifts so make yourself available if someone comes knocking on your door.

This is also an excellent period in which to give some quality time to your children if you are a parent. To those of you working 100 hours a week with every excuse under the Sun for not being available for your children, it might be timely to set aside a few lines in your diary for your kids. You'll be glad you did because these planets indicate a wealth of pleasure and joy interacting with youngsters.

Mercury and Uranus offer you incredibly quick responses around the 9th. An opportunity should be seized without too much thinking as this promises to deliver some wonderful benefits to you, not only materially but mentally and emotionally. Of course, it's important to do work that enriches your soul not just your bank account.

If you've wanted to make a break and move into a direction that fulfils you much more professionally, you can do so at this time. Again, seize the opportunity if it's presented, even doesn't seem as if there is much to it at first. You'll be pleased you did. Don't let your mistrust of the bringer of your good news cause you to miss a valuable opportunity.

You can find yourself working much better with someone with whom you previously had issues around the 13th. What this effectively means is that your mind is clear and you can focus more on the job at hand rather than strategising and having to deal with personalities. This can make you so much more productive and happy at work.

The Sun moves to the important eighth zone of your horoscope on the 21st, indicating a greater focus on your shared resources. You may find yourself having some problems agreeing on a joint monetary project either at home or in the workplace, particularly if you are a business owner. By the 30th an understanding can be reached.

Romance and friendship

This month continues to be very energetic for you and particularly after the 4th you'll need to hang out with people who are as upbeat as yourself. If you find yourself in a rut with those who are trying to dampen your spirits, you're likely to lock horns. Don't be afraid to expand your circle of influence this month.

Although a romantic relationship may be winding down by the 6th, it doesn't necessarily mean that this person will leave your life completely. If the ending is amicable, you will still maintain a good relationship with this person because your karmic bonds are strong and there are still many lessons that you can learn from each other. The trick of exiting a relationship is to maintain the friendship.

The benefits of rendering a service to someone on the 9th will be more beneficial to your future than you think. You will not necessarily be doing yourself a favour because of what you will receive in return, but your kindness will not be forgotten and will come back as a bonus sometime in the future. Try to avoid gossip on the 18th as someone you trust may have a hidden agenda.

Party hard between the 22nd and 29th because it will be all work and no play in the coming weeks. However, if you exhaust yourself too much, you will be hard pressed to find the energy you need in executing your duties. Pace yourself as this doesn't necessarily mean you can't still have lots of fun along the way. Your social popularity continues.

You need to come to the rescue of a sibling or neighbour who is having problems around the 30th. It's best to do this on neutral territory as it could be easy for you to get sucked into the drama of their life. Maintaining emotional distance yet at the same time being of assistance requires a delicate balance on your part. You'll be of great help to them by remaining emotionally aloof.

Work and money

You can kill two birds with one stone this month as business and pleasure mix quite well for you during June. Around the 3rd a friend or lover could be instrumental in helping you secure a better financial position or will at least steer you in the right direction.

The 7th is a powerful time of the month to shine and put your best foot forward. Your creative enterprises will be met with a warm reception and even concepts that seem a little far-fetched will actually be seen as having some practical merit as well. Between the 14th and 21st changes on the work front could be exasperating but will be well worth it if you persist.

Tidying up a lot of private business will be high on your agenda and between the 26th and 28th you can make reasonable headway in these matters. Communication with a distant work colleague or someone who can provide you with a solution to a financial issue is likely between the 29th and the 30th as well. Meditation and yoga are not a bad idea, either, if you're feeling a little stressed out from work and deadlines.

Positive: 7, 9, 13, 22, 23, 24, 25, 26, 27, 28, 29

Negative: 1, 2, 5, 6

Mixed: 3, 4, 14, 15, 16, 17, 18, 19, 20, 21, 30

Highlights of the month

During the month of July you mustn't let your imagination run away with you. You're likely to think the worst of yourself and others due to your powerful visualisations. Imagination can be used either positively or negatively so try to direct this energy in ways that can uplift your moments rather than destroy them.

In the first week of the month, particularly between the 1st and the 3rd, you're likely to feel at odds with what you want professionally and what is available. You will experience considerable frustration if you had been promised a new position or better workplace conditions only to find these are delayed. Exercise patience and don't think the worst.

During this same first week of July the position of Venus and Neptune caution you do not look at the world through rose-coloured glasses. You may make some miscalculations or rather misjudgements about the character of others and, if you happen to be newly introduced to someone, don't jump the gun and assume that they are everything you initially would like to believe. Spend a little time getting to know them before drawing your conclusions.

Although the month gets off to a shaky start romantically, the entry of Venus into your marriage sign is extraordinarily lucky and satisfying. Some Sagittarians who are of marriage-able age are likely to tie the knot or least make some plans along these lines.

The other possibility is that someone you know either socially or a relative is likely to given some accolade or award and you will be invited to take part in the grand celebrations. Because Mars and Jupiter create some unfavourable aspect at this time and have an influence on your zone of travels, it would be a shame if you can't attend the function due to a factor of distance. Be a step ahead of these issues if you sense there may be an offer to travel on the table.

Your hard work pays off this month between the 9th and the 15th and you are likely to receive at least a pat on the back for persisting with a rather troublesome workload. Your bril-liant ideas and dedicated work will be recognised by those higher up.

Educational pursuits are spotlighted after the 23rd and, if you're sitting through exams or looking to improve your skill set in some way, the period after the 25th indicates even better success for you. This might be your ticket to an increased weekly salary or bonus. Having a degree or diploma under your belt will soon help you at some point.

Romance and friendship

Friends will be demanding this month and you'll need to be on your best behaviour as far as they are concerned. This could limit your autonomy and freedom of speech, which will result in you exploding after suppressing your feelings for too long on the 1st. Focus on long-term relationship objectives. News surrounding a good friend after the 6th is inspiring.

You have to be careful In how you express yourself between the 2nd and the 5th, particularly if you happen to be in the company of those older and more conservative in their views. Sometime after the 7th you could also find yourself needing to revamp your philosophical skills to keep up with a rather in-depth conversation.

Between the 13th and 17th you're amorous and should attract a new romance, but if you are already attached it could present some problems. The proverbial 'love triangle' is looming and you need to nip this in the bud before it gets out of hand. Issues of trust regarding your partner or a friend will also weigh heavily upon you, particularly around the 20th.

On the 28th, the harder you try to remember something, the more you'll forget it. The reverse can sometimes true, which is, try to forget whatever you can't remember and it's likely that, when you least expect it, it will come to mind again. You'll be trying to cast your memory back in time to an event that somehow may have shaped your destiny. This event was a long time ago and may have gotten lost in the million other thought processes in your mind. Don't worry, you will eventually remember.

Work and money

Your dilemma between the 4th and the 8th has to do with becoming more financially robust and disciplined, but your desire to continue spending is still strong. Think of the benefits of self-control and frugality. You have to re-train your mind into believing that less is more and, although this will be hard in the first instance, as the old saying goes, 'Practice makes perfect'. You too can become an expert at being tight-fisted.

Around the 15th you'll kick yourself if you spend a lot of money on a training course or some other activity that leaves you high and dry when you actually get there. What will you do? Do the proper thing and leave so that you can enjoy your life doing something else. Don't waste a minute, I say, and certainly don't look back on a simple mistake of having spent money on something which you realise is not going to be of any lasting benefit to you.

It is 'Out with the old and in with the new' between the 20th and the 24th. Get rid of outdated gadgets, furniture and other stuff that no longer works for you. Just as technology moves forward with time, so should you embrace new techniques in dealing with life. Don't be afraid to enjoy this challenge of growth.

Positive: 9, 10, 11, 12, 20, 21, 22, 23, 24, 25

Negative: 1, 2, 3, 4, 5, 8, 28

Mixed: 6, 7, 13, 14, 15, 16, 17

Highlights of the month

Things move at a hectic pace throughout August so you must be careful to curb your desire for more and more. With Venus entering your zone of sex, spiritual regeneration and anything deep and mysterious, you may also want plenty of these things as well. You must adjust yourself to the level of desire of those around you.

At the same time Mars and Venus will switch on all your 'hot' buttons and this could find you involved in some sexual affair or relationship, one which is based purely on lust rather than friendship and deeper values. How emotionally mature you are will soon be seen by you and others. Difficulties in current relationships are also not out of the question and the first few days of the month will certainly be a test.

You will resist change at this time and will need ample proof of the benefits of doing something in someone else's way. The point really is that you may not be attentive enough to the benefits of what the other person has to offer you and could miss an opportunity or two this month. However, it is likely that by the 11th you'll be more receptive to what is on the table and will benefit from the suggestions of others.

You need to keep a hold on valuable papers and documents this month and particularly around the 15th you are likely to mishandle paperwork or something valuable. Try to get your filing and organisation systems in order easily so that you can recollect where everything is.

The other issue at this time is that you may entrust some of your work or confidential material to someone who is not on the ball as much as you are. This might create a situation where the job has to be redone and you'll get egg on your face. Make sure the skills and credentials of those whom you give your work are up to a reasonable standard.

After the 16th you must be on guard not to overspend lavishly, even if you think you need something. The temptation is to buy things that will later sit around and collect dust. Re-evaluate what important at this stage in your life and you'll soon learn that most of what you desire is not really essential. Restrict your spending to things that are of practical use to you.

By the last week of August, particularly between the 25th and 30th, you'll get an extra dose of self-confidence to help you get things done. Make sure you get out and blow off a little bit of steam so you can handle the Sun's and Mars' energy coming your way.

Romance and friendship

This is a perfect time to weed out half-hearted acquaintances from your peer group of true friends. Between the 4th and the 10th you can forge a deeper tie with someone whom you had recently only superficially just begun to know. This new friendship will bring you joy and is likely to continue well into the future. You can learn something about your financial situation by your association with this person as well.

You mustn't hang on to the experiences or the people that come as part of the package deal of life between the 11th and

17th. People will come and go but the wisdom you have learned from these challenges will hold you in good stead.

You're entering an intense romantic phase. Around the 19th your love life could throw you a few spin balls, which could rattle you to the core if you don't brace yourself and get prepared for the inevitable changes that life brings in love affairs.

You will push relationships to the limit between the 24th and 27th; but, are you prepared to be pushed to the same level by the other person? You have to take as good as you give if you want your love life to grow strongly.

About the 30th you will feel a spiritual elevation that will give you a brand new set of insights—tools if you will—which you can use in your everyday life as well.

Work and money

You'll do something you haven't investigated thoroughly enough on the 7th. There are pros and cons to any venture and the plan you have may be a little lopsided. You may have already been warned by someone close to you about the pitfalls but your pride may get in the road of listening to their good counsel.

The rules of the game are changing and you could be caught out if you think you're on top of a particular task or commitment you've given someone. On the 11th you will find that there's more to the job than you had at first envisaged and you could have left yourself short on time completing this demand. You need to be doubly efficient with your time and resources so that you can prove you are up to the task.

Work gets a more hectic between the 18th and the 22nd, so don't think that you can slacken off. This would be a mistake and could leave you in an embarrassing situation with an employer or co-worker. Speak to them early and look at your timeline so that you can see where the gaps are in your diary ahead of time.

Positive: 4, 5, 6, 8, 9, 10, 12, 13, 14, 17, 28, 29, 30

Negative: 18, 19, 20, 21, 22, 19, 24

Mixed: 7, 11, 15, 16, 25, 26, 27

Highlights of the month

Your excellent networking and social contacts can help you climb the ladder of success in September but, as most successful people will tell you, it isn't always an easy ride to the top. This month, with the Sun entering into the proximity of Saturn, you'll have your work cut out for you.

If you're good at your job—and it's quite likely that this is the case—others will be looking to offload their surplus work on you so that they are the ones who have an easy ride. If you become too sensitive about saying 'No' to their requests, you'll be the one regretting long hours and tedious work deadlines because you didn't speak up. Between the 2nd and the 11th these planetary demands become more intense, that's for sure.

Power plays are likely to be a key ingredient in your life mix this month because of Mercury and Pluto demanding a diplomatic turn of phrase from you, especially around the 17th. Buying into others' ego tripping will be hard to sidestep but this must be done if you are to remain peaceful in your working environment.

Fortunately Venus entering the 10th sign of your career activities softens the blow and makes you able to deflect these problems elsewhere onto someone else. Try to remain a little invisible if someone is on your case. Mix your business with pleasure this month and positive results will surely be yours by the 21st.

Your social life will also cut you a little relief after the 24th when group activities are again a whole lot more fun. By getting involved in community based activities or possibly even charitable works your mind will be taken to another level and this will help you forget some of your own cares and worries.

Brilliant if not dazzling circumstances can be expected after the 25th with Mercury and Uranus offering you a whole new lease of life, particularly regarding your mental ideas. A friend might give you a hint that inspires you to go further in your job, using a hobby you've pursued for some time. The worst-case scenario is that you may suddenly have to put pen to paper to put someone in their place if they've sent you an e-mail or made a telephone call and erroneously accused you of something.

If you feel awkward or dissatisfied with your look at this time, it might be opportune to get a new hairstyle, new look, or simply to step out of your old self and see what's possible. This is a period of experimentation with who you are.

Romance and friendship

Dust yourself down on the 3rd if you've been through a rather difficult time emotionally because the peak of stress is now over and you can relax more. This doesn't mean you should let down your guard but you can now get on with enjoying life a little more rather than feeling as if you have to lock horns with those whom you feel most intimately connected

You could be torn between two courses of action based upon your ethics between the 6th and 11th. Circumstances sometimes don't clearly define the correct protocol of how to act or speak, especially if it is a first-time occasion. If you do happen to be invited somewhere a little out of the ordinary, get the heads up on how others in the same position would best deal with a situation like this. It will have to do with your attire as much as your intellectual or communication skills.

You will not approve of the behaviour of a friend around the 14th but will need to be particularly careful as to how you address the issue. You could be feeling embarrassed by someone's verbal or fashion expression and need to say something about it otherwise it could impact upon your own self-respect.

You're in your own element after the 22nd and, even if others don't approve of the way you do things, you will know that you are right and should stick to your guns. The old saying that may apply to your life in this respect is, 'If it ain't broke, don't fix it'. You may be trying to find a reason to change things for no valid cause. On the 23rd this could create confusion and make life harder for all concerned.

Work and money

You need to show some goodwill in a situation and not count the dollars or cents, especially if you're expending a bit more time and energy than you had expected. A charitable deed will not go unnoticed, even though this is not the main reason to do a favour for someone. Just remember, karma does come back around and you'll be rewarded for your compassionate gesture on the 2nd, 7th and 11th.

You mustn't let confusion or an inability to understand a mathematical or financial line of thinking to dictate a monetary transaction on the 15th or 16th. If you're dealing with salespeople or those more experienced in their understanding of how money works, you need to give yourself some additional time to understand their logic fully. They will be trying to pull the wool over your eyes as well.

Doing a complete makeover on your house or apartment doesn't require much money. It might simply require a good clean and de-clutter to create the same effect. If you're pushed for space and need more storage area, you'd be surprised at how much junk you've accumulated over the years. Try doing an early spring clean between the 24th and 30th to see the difference it makes.

Positive: 21, 22, 24, 25, 26, 27, 28, 29, 30

Negative: 3, 4, 5, 6, 8, 9, 10, 14, 15, 16, 17, 23

Mixed: 2, 7, 11

Highlights of the month

It's time to balance your need for wealth is and an excellent lifestyle with your heart's desires for a career that offers work satisfaction. Venus, Mercury and Saturn join forces in your career zone this month and this is very significant.

There's no doubt you will have the get up and go to achieve fine results financially; but the important question is, are you really satisfied with what you're doing? Have you reached that point in your life where you wish you could be doing what you love but secretly fear the gamble may not earn you as much as you are accustomed to? These are the questions that will be uppermost in your mind during October and particularly between the 4th and the 9th you will need to assess carefully which fork in the road of your life you want to take.

Friends will be a great support under these planetary transits and, when Mercury enters your zone of friendship after the 10th, people who are even only casually acquainted with you could become more closely involved in your affairs. Someone you had possibly thought would never endear themselves to you will now play an important role in your life.

Your love affairs may not be quite as fulfilling due to the alliance of Venus and Saturn but it is an opportunity for you to get more practical with the one you love and talk about what you want to talk as a couple. Between the 13th and the 16th you'll need to overlook each other's human frailties and love each other simply for who you are. Unconditional love will be a test for you and those other meaningful people in your life.

Even though you get the green light on some project after the 18th, you could feel a little frazzled and may need to postpone the whole thing. You will, however, be quite pleased that a mini promotion could be in store for you and you'll be well remunerated for it. Giving yourself some tender loving attention by the 29th will be essential for you to recharge your batteries.

Saturn makes an all important transition out of your zone of career and into that of friendships on the 30th. This is a significant shift in your life and introduces a new two-and-a-half-year cycle.

Romance and friendship

Some of your dreams will come true between the 4th and 8th. Pay attention to what is being thrown up from your subconscious because this may offer you vital clues as to how you should live your life. Make a dream diary and note down your feelings and visions during your sleep. There will be some very powerful revelations.

Your plans could be at odds with your partner or a friend between the 9th and 14th, particularly if this relates to travel. Before disputing the agenda, why not separately write down what you feel is your preferred list of destinations and activities and then share your ideas with each other in a cordial fashion? This way you'll avoid conflict and can achieve a win–win situation for a knockout show for all concerned.

Your sexual responses will be all-important in determining the mode of your relationships on the 13th, 16th and 23rd. You could be afraid that your level of affection or demonstrativeness is either not sufficient or not in keeping with what your partner desires. You're never going to know unless you communicate your concerns about this and get your partner to share their feelings in the same way.

The 29th or 30th could be one of those days where you're waiting for a call or visit from a friend. You might have been certain that the plans were clearly agreed upon. Unfortunately it may not be that simple. There could be a miscommunication which will cause you to be waiting around quite a while and possibly even feeling agitated that they had forgotten or completely crossed you off the list completely. Don't jump to conclusions, however.

Work and money

When it rains it pours and your professional life will offer you a series of difficult choices around the 8th just as you thought the year was coming to a close. It's probably best to hold off making any important decision, even if a position or job prospect seems overly attractive. If you can wait you'll make the right judgement.

You'll feel confident about your monetary situation between the 13th and 16th but you shouldn't have any false illusions of just how costly things can be. For this reason continue to be a little more frugal rather than blowing your money on useless necessities. It's the thought that counts so don't think for a moment that you need to spend big to prove how you feel about someone.

Between the 25th and 30th you'll enter a lucky period, which provides you with fortunate meetings and opportunities. It's just as easy to negotiate a large deal as it is to fritter away your time on smaller issues. Think big and shoot for the sky.

Positive: 15, 16, 23, 18, 25, 26, 27, 28

Negative: 11, 12

Mixed: 4, 5, 6, 7, 8, 9, 10, 13, 14, 29, 30

Highlights of the month

You'll be thankful for the clarity of mind you experience as November a gets underway. You'll be more settled and clearer in your sense of purpose and generally will also have a greater sense of gratitude for your life and the world. Luck is in the air between the 2nd and the 5th and you'll also want to share some of your gains with those you consider worthy.

Negotiations seem to go quiet for you but don't count your chickens before they hatch. You are possibly a spendthrift this month and will want to surround yourself with luxuries, eat the best food, drink the best wine and drive the fastest cars.

There's a limit to your budget, you know that, so do be a little more mindful of where the dollars and cents are going. You might be seriously tempted to engage in some retail therapy between the 8th and the 11th. Be careful and if necessary tear up your credit cards before they get the better of you.

This month will also require you to assess carefully and balance your needs and the needs of others. If for the sake of gaining Brownie points you become a victim when bending over backwards for others, it could be time to think about what you want, even if that puts a few noses out of joint. Mercury and Neptune will bring this point to the fore sometime around the 12th.

Disapproving authorities such as your boss can make it difficult for you to work. It's not easy when someone is breathing down your neck, nitpicking every single detail of what you know you can do quite well. You'll falter if someone is highlighting your weaknesses day after day. You'll need to have a powwow with someone between the 14th and the 16th.

Your confidence may not be serving you all that well after the 22nd and a refresher course in your chosen line of study or work wouldn't be a bad idea. This doesn't necessarily mean you must re-enrol in a course of education but it's not a bad idea to be armed with the facts and sharpen your wits before entering any important meetings this month. Someone might try to belittle you in some way, so be prepared.

Romance and friendship

You need excitement and to be around people who are as revved up as yourself. Between the 2nd and 8th you may meet someone who really stimulates and inspires you romantically. One of your closest friends will not approve but this won't matter as you realise you must live life on your own terms. This is a very active period for you.

You will be taking more interest in bioethical issues and the topic of global warming. On the 9th you'll find unique and novel ways to do your part to reduce greenhouse emissions and also contribute less to the general pollution that we are now experiencing in the world. Your intuition is also strong between the 6th and 8th, so trust that.

A disagreement with a friend will leave you a little down in the dumps or at least physically lethargic around the 16th or 17th. However, your energies will pick up when some level-headed communications lift your spirits and mend the rift.

It doesn't matter whether or not people want to help you with the project or chores around the house on the 12th because you will demand their assistance in any case. Between the 15th and 19th, if you have lazy children hanging around the house that aren't pulling their weight, this could be a case in point. Don't pull any punches and the job will get done.

On the 24th, the 26th and 27th your passion may not meet with the same reciprocal level of intensity as you have expected but this requires patience on your part. On the 30th this situation will change so don't throw the baby out with the bathwater. You're emotional as well, so do some extra physical exercise this week.

Work and money

Between the 1st and the 8th you won't be able to decide whether spending money will give you the mental relief you need or if you'll regret it afterwards. It's probably better to wait till after the second half of the month to splurge on yourself. By then you'll have a clearer picture of your budgetary requirements.

Between the 9th and the 12th, seek out a new job or purchase that new property that has taken your fancy. The Sun and Mercury offer you perfect networking opportunities. Go hard at it if you are interested in making some lifestyle change before the month is out.

You'll probably want to get your books out early to get a head start on your studies as 2009 nears the finishing line. But your heart may simply not be in it. Get into some fun between the 17th and the 25th so you can get it out of your system before you get back into work mode. You can achieve some good things professionally if you try.

This needn't be an intense and emotionally trying time at work. There may possibly be disputes with those whom you work if you don't keep your reactions in check, but this needn't be so. Income tax, alimony, or joint finances could also be at the heart of domestic disagreements. Your financial focus is quite strong between the 26th and the 29th but your partner may have different ideas.

Positive: 25, 30

Negative: 22

Mixed: 1, 2, 3, 4, 5, 6, 7, 8, 9, 10, 11, 12, 14, 15, 16, 17, 18, 19, 24, 26, 27, 28, 29

DECEMBER

Highlights of the month

It's not a bad idea to get that medical check-up at this late stage of the year just to nip in the bud any of those minor ailments that might knock you out leading up to Christmas. It's also perhaps timely to increase your fibre intake and pay more attention to the calibre of food that you are eating. Diet will play an important role in increasing your vitality and fitness this month.

Usually people wind down at the end of the year, readying themselves for holidays and parties, but you'll be firing on all eight cylinders with brilliant new ideas for the coming year. Between the 1st and the 7th you might even want to solidify some of those plans so that you get off to a great head start in 2010.

A last-minute dash to the finishing line with your finances is indicated around the 8th and 9th. Apply some of your clever ingenuity to tidying up loose ends with tax and possibly other work-related pay issues. Don't be shy in coming forward if you feel there is something amiss.

Holidays may come early for you this year because the Sun stimulates you to get away from everything and make up lost leisure time. This is more likely if you're able to put those previous tasks to bed prior to the 14th.

Between the 17th and the 25th you will experience a great deal of camaraderie and family closeness, which will make this a wonderful Christmas period for you. The saucy combination of Venus and Mars again brings you into the limelight of love and sexual opportunity. Because you're likely to be relaxed, this will also be a source of great pleasure and stimulation, not just physically but mentally and emotionally, too.

A challenge for the year comes from the reverse motion of Mars at a time when you might be preparing for a wonderful holiday and preparing for fun. Just around the 21st you might discover that you haven't quite finished off some chore or job and this could leave you feeling worried and possibly even anxious. There may be nothing you can do about it so my sincere suggestion for you is to sort this out after the holiday period; switch off your mind for the moment and really enjoy the remainder of 2009.

You have high expectations for your romantic potential in the coming months and the final cherry on top of the cake will be your positive view of love and your ability to find happiness in this sphere. Relationships should be intense but fulfilling at the close of this exciting year.

Romance and friendship

Venus will move to your Sun sign on the 2nd. This is always a great omen and marks the beginning of a very amorous cycle for you. Your energy levels are high and your emotional and sexual self-confidence just as strong. Use this time to foster relationships as much as possible. You should feel really great up until the 11th.

Between the 4th and 7th you'll be feeling much more optimistic than usual and this will have a positive impact on every aspect of your life. In fact, some of your friends will wonder if something is wrong. Believe it or not this is the way you should naturally feel and it's not a bad idea to dig deeply to see precisely what has caused such a particularly good mood.

You could feel apprehensive about travelling with someone but they may be forcing the issue around the 9th. You need to convince them of your limits, even though you know full well that you have reached the end your tether. This could take a little bit of convincing on your part but will be well worth it if you can bring the person in question around to your way of thinking.

You have some good stuff going on astrologically on the 20th but you mustn't let others subject you to their own negative influences. Cutting off someone who has been a bad influence is long overdue. Your conscience will feel much clearer once you take the inevitable step around this time and say goodbye.

Who said you can't have your cake and eat it, too? Between the 26th and 30th, fortune smiles on you, making you attempt to do a few things you might not have done before. Socially speaking this gives you the advantage when your name will be on everyone's lips. Well, you may just get your five minutes of fame after all!

Work and money

You will lose your drive now to achieve anything worthwhile and could blame it on others. Between the 8th and 16th don't let this attitude overtake you, even though a little good cheer is justifiable. Collect your energies and be prepared to get back into the slipstream of hard work for just a few more days until the Christmas festivities begin.

After the 20th you may need to reassess the nature of the work you are doing to see whether or not you are earning what you deserve. There's no point complaining that you're not getting ahead and can't save enough money. You are responsible for where you are and can change things if you want.

Earnestness and fearlessness are the two traits for propelling yourself forward out of a situation you aren't satisfied with.

The 28th is a creative sort of day so doesn't waste it on useless activities that aren't going to give you happiness. You will feel distracted by people who don't really have anything better to other than to while away the time. You can produce good work, so spend it alone if you have to.

Positive: 1, 2, 3, 4, 5, 6, 7, 17, 18, 19, 21, 22, 23, 24, 25, 26, 27, 28, 29, 30

Negative: 21

Mixed: 8, 9, 10, 11, 12, 13, 14, 15, 16, 20

2009:
Astronumerology

Name is a fence and within it you are nameless.

—Samuli Paronen

The power behind your name

By adding the numbers of your name you can see which planet is ruling you. Each of the letters of the alphabet is assigned a number, which is tabled below. These numbers are ruled by the planets. This is according to the ancient Chaldean system of numerology and is very different to the Pythagorean system to which many refer.

Each number is assigned a planet:

AIQJY	=	1	Sun
BKR	=	2	Moon
CGLS	=	3	Jupiter
DMT	=	4	Uranus
EHNX	=	5	Mercury
UVW	=	6	Venus
OZ	=	7	Neptune
FP	=	8	Saturn
—	=	9	Mars

Notice that the number 9 is not allotted a letter because it is considered special. Once the numbers have been added you will see that a single planet rules your name and personal affairs. Many famous actors, writers and musicians change their names to attract the energy of a luckier planet. You can experiment with the table and try new names or add letters of your second name to see how that vibration suits you. It's a lot of fun!

Here is an example of how to find out the power of your name. If your name is John Smith, calculate the ruling planet by correlating each letter to a number in the table like this:

J O H N   S M I T H

1 7 5 5   3 4 1 4 5

Now add the numbers like this:

1 + 7 + 5 + 5 + 3 + 4 + 1 + 4 + 5 = 35

Then add 3 + 5 = 8

The ruling number of John Smith's name is 8, which is ruled by Saturn. Now study the name-number table to reveal the power of your name. The numbers 3 and 5 will also play a secondary role in John's character and destiny so in this case you would also study the effects of Jupiter and Mercury.

Name-number table

Your name number	Ruling planet	Your name characteristics
1	Sun	Charismatic personality. Great vitality and life force. Physically active and outgoing. Attracts good friends and individuals in powerful positions. Good government connections. Intelligent, dramatic, showy and successful. A loyal number for relationships.
2	Moon	Soft, emotional temperament. Changeable moods but psychic, intuitive senses. Imaginative nature and compassionate expression of feelings. Loves family, mother and home life. Night owl who probably needs more sleep.

Success with the public and/or the opposite sex.

3	Jupiter	Outgoing, optimistic number with lucky overtones. Attracts opportunities without trying. Good sense of timing. Religious or spiritual aspirations. Can investigate the meaning of life. Loves to travel and explore the world and people.
4	Uranus	Explosive personality with many quirky aspects. Likes the untried and untested. Forward thinking, with many unusual friends. Gets bored easily so needs plenty of stimulating experiences. Innovative, technological and creative. Wilful and stubborn when wants to be. Unexpected events in life may be positive or negative.
5	Mercury	Quick-thinking mind with great powers of speech. Extremely active life; always on the go and lives on nervous energy. Youthful attitude and never grows old. Looks younger than actual age. Young friends and humorous disposition. Loves reading and writing.
6	Venus	Charming personality. Graceful and attractive character, who cherishes friends and social life. Musical or artistic interests. Good for money making as well as numerous love affairs. Career in

the public eye is possible. Loves family but is often overly concerned by friends.

7	Neptune	Intuitive, spiritual and self-sacrificing nature. Easily duped by those who need help. Loves to dream of life's possibilities. Has healing powers. Dreams are revealing and prophetic. Loves the water and will have many journeys in life. Spiritual aspirations dominate worldly desires.
8	Saturn	Hard-working, focused individual with slow but certain success. Incredible concentration and self-sacrifice for a goal. Money orientated but generous when trust is gained. Professional but may be a hard taskmaster. Demands highest standards and needs to learn to enjoy life a little more.
9	Mars	Incredible physical drive and ambition. Sports and outdoor activities are keys to health. Combative and likes to work and play just as hard. Protective of family, friends and territory. Individual tastes in life but is also self-absorbed. Needs to listen to others' advice to gain greater success.

Your 2009 planetary ruler

Astrology and numerology are closely linked. Each planet rules over a number between 1 and 9. Both your name and your birth date are ruled by planetary energies. Here are the planets and their ruling numbers:

1 Sun; 2 Moon; 3 Jupiter; 4 Uranus; 5 Mercury; 6 Venus; 7 Neptune; 8 Saturn; 9 Mars

Simply add the numbers of your birth date and the year in question to find out which planet will control the coming year for you. Here is an example:

If you were born on 12 November, add the numerals 1 and 2 (12, your day of birth) and 1 and 1 (11, your month of birth) to the year in question, in this case 2009 (current year), like this:

Add $1 + 2 + 1 + 1 + 2 + 0 + 0 + 9 = 16$

Then add these numbers again: $1 + 6 = 7$

The planet ruling your individual karma for 2009 will be Neptune because this planet rules the number 7.

You can even take your ruling name number as shown above and add it to the year in question to throw more light on your coming personal affairs like this:

John Smith = 8

Year coming = 2009

Add $8 + 2 + 0 + 0 + 9 = 19$

Add $1 + 9 = 10$

Add $1 + 0 = 1$

This is the ruling year number using your name number as a basis. Therefore, study the Sun's (number 1) influence for 2009. Enjoy!

1 = Year of the Sun

Overview

The Sun is the brightest object in the heavens and rules number 1 and the sign of Leo. Because of this the coming year will bring you great success and popularity.

You'll be full of life and radiant vibrations and are more than ready to tackle your new nine-year cycle, which begins now. Any new projects you commence are likely to be successful.

Your health and vitality will be very strong and your stamina at its peak. Even if you happen to have the odd problem with your health, your recuperative power will be strong.

You have tremendous magnetism this year so social popularity won't be a problem for you. I see many new friends and lovers coming into your life. Expect loads of invitations to parties and fun-filled outings. Just don't take your health for granted as you're likely to burn the candle at both ends.

With success coming your way, don't let it go to your head. You must maintain humility, which will make you even more popular in the coming year.

Love and pleasure

This is an important cycle for renewing your love and connections with your family, particularly if you have children. The Sun is connected with the sign of Leo and therefore brings an increase in musical and theatrical activities. Entertainment and other creative hobbies will be high on your agenda and bring you a great sense of satisfaction.

Work

You won't have to make too much effort to be successful this year as the brightness of the Sun will draw opportunities to you. Changes in work are likely and if you have been concerned that opportunities are few and far between, 2009 will be different. You can expect some sort of promotion or an increase in income because your employers will take special note of your skills and service orientation.

Improving your luck

Leo is the ruler of number 1 and therefore, if you're born under this star sign, 2009 will be particularly lucky. For others, July and August, the months of Leo, will bring good fortune. The 1st, 8th, 15th and 22nd hours of Sundays especially will give you a unique sort of luck in any sort of competition or activities generally. Keep your eye out for those born under Leo as they may be able to contribute something to your life and may even have a karmic connection to you. This is a particularly important year for your destiny.

Your lucky numbers in this coming cycle are 1, 10, 19 and 28.

2 = Year of the Moon

Overview

There's nothing more soothing than the cool light of the full Moon on a clear night. The Moon is emotional and receptive and controls your destiny in 2009. If you're able to use the positive energies of the Moon, it will be a great year in which you can realign and improve your relationships, particularly with family members.

Making a commitment to becoming a better person and bringing your emotions under control will also dominate your thinking. Try not to let your emotions get the better of you throughout the coming year because you may be drawn into the changeable nature of these lunar vibrations as well. If you fail to keep control of your emotional life you'll later regret some of your actions. You must carefully blend thinking with feeling to arrive at the best results. Your luck throughout 2009 will certainly be determined by the state of your mind.

Because the Moon and the sign of Cancer rule the number 2 there is a certain amount of change to be expected this year. Keep your feelings steady and don't let your heart rule your head.

Love and pleasure

Your primary concern in 2009 will be your home and family life. You'll be keen to finally take on those renovations, or work on your garden. You may even think of buying a new home. You can at last carry out some of those plans and make your dreams come true. If you find yourself a little more temperamental than usual, do some extra meditation and spend time alone until you sort this out. You mustn't withhold your feelings from your partner as this will only create frustration.

Work

During 2009 your focus will be primarily on feelings and family; however, this doesn't mean you can't make great strides in your work as well. The Moon rules the general public and what you might find is that special opportunities and connections with the world at large present themselves to you. You could be working with large numbers of people.

If you're looking for a better work opportunity, try to focus your attention on women who can give you a hand. Use your intuition as it will be finely tuned this year. Work and career success depends upon your instincts.

Improving your luck

The sign of Cancer is your ruler this year and because the Moon rules Mondays, both this day of the week and the month of July are extremely lucky for you. The 1st, 8th, 15th and 22nd hours on Mondays will be very powerful. Pay special attention to the new and full Moon days throughout 2009.

The numbers 2, 11 and 29 are lucky for you.

3 = Year of Jupiter

Overview

The year 2009 will be a 3 year for you and, because of this, Jupiter and Sagittarius will dominate your affairs. This is very lucky and shows that you'll be motivated to broaden your horizons, gain more money and become extremely popular in your social circles. It looks like 2009 will be a fun-filled year with much excitement.

Jupiter and Sagittarius are generous to a fault and so likewise, your openhandedness will mark the year. You'll be friendly and helpful to all of those around you.

Pisces is also under the rulership of the number 3 and this brings out your spiritual and compassionate nature. You'll become a much better person, reducing your negative karma by increasing your self-awareness and spiritual feelings. You will want to share your luck with those you love.

Love and pleasure

Travel and seeking new adventures will be part and parcel of your romantic life this year. Travelling to distant lands and meeting unusual people will open your heart to fresh possibilities of romance.

You'll try novel and audacious things and will find yourself in a different circle of friends. Compromise will be important in making your existing relationships work. Talk about your feelings. If you are currently in a relationship you'll feel an upswing in your affection for them. This is a perfect opportunity to deepen your love for each other and take your relationship to a new level.

If you're not yet attached to someone just yet, there's good news for you. Great opportunities lie in store for you and a spiritual or karmic connection may be experienced in 2009.

Work

Great fortune can be expected through your working life in the next twelve months. Your friends and work colleagues will want to help you achieve your goals. Even your employers will be amenable to your requests for extra money or a better position within the organisation.

If you want to start a new job or possibly begin an independent line of business this is a great year to do it. Jupiter looks set to give you plenty of opportunities, success and a superior reputation.

Improving your luck

As long as you can keep a balanced view of things and not overdo anything, your luck will increase dramatically throughout 2009. The important thing is to remain grounded and not be too airy-fairy about your objectives. Be realistic about your talents and capabilities and don't brag about your skills or achievements. This will only invite envy from others.

Moderate your social life as well and don't drink or eat too much as this will slow your reflexes and lessen your chances for success.

You have plenty of spiritual insights this year so you should use them to their maximum. In the 1st, 8th, 15th and 24th hours of Thursdays you should use your intuition to enhance your luck, and the numbers 3, 12, 21 and 30 are also lucky for you. March and December are your lucky months but generally the whole year should go pretty smoothly for you.

4 = Year of Uranus

Overview

The electric and exciting planet of the zodiac Uranus and its sign of Aquarius rule your affairs throughout 2009. Dramatic events will surprise and at the same time unnerve you in your professional and personal life. So be prepared!

You'll be able to achieve many things this year and your dreams are likely to come true, but you mustn't be distracted or scattered with your energies. You'll be breaking through your own self-limitations and this will present challenges from your family and friends. You'll want to be independent and develop your spiritual powers and nothing will stop you.

Try to maintain discipline and an orderly lifestyle so you can make the most of these special energies this year. If unexpected things do happen, it's not a bad idea to have an alternative plan so you don't lose momentum.

Work

Technology, computing and the Internet will play a larger role in your professional life this coming year. You'll have to move ahead with the times and learn new skills if you want to achieve success.

A hectic schedule is likely, so make sure your diary is with you at all times. Try to be more efficient and don't waste time.

New friends and alliances at work will help you achieve even greater success in the coming period. Becoming a team player will be even more important towards gaining satisfaction in your professional endeavours.

Love and pleasure

You want something radical, something different in your relationships this year. It's quite likely that your love life will be feeling a little less than exciting so you'll take some important steps to change that. If your partner is as progressive as you'll be this year, then your relationship is likely to improve and fulfil both of you.

In your social life you will meet some very unusual people whom you'll feel are specially connected to you spiritually. You may want to ditch everything for the excitement and passion of a completely new relationship, but tread carefully as this may not work out exactly as you'd expected.

Improving your luck

Moving too quickly and impulsively will cause you problems on all fronts, so be a little more patient and think your decisions through more carefully. Social, romantic and professional opportunities will come to you but take a little time to investigate the ramifications of your actions.

The 1st, 8th, 15th and 20th hours of any Saturday are lucky, but love and luck are likely to cross your path when you least expect it. The numbers 4, 13, 22 and 31 are also lucky for you this year.

5 = Year of Mercury

Overview

The supreme planet of communication, Mercury, is your ruling planet throughout 2009. The number 5, which is connected to Mercury, will confer upon you success through your intellectual abilities.

Any form of writing or speaking will be improved and this will be, to a large extent, underpinning your success. Your imagination will be stimulated by this planet with many incredible new and exciting ideas will come to mind.

Mercury and the number 5 are considered somewhat indecisive. Be firm in your attitude and don't let too many ideas or opportunities distract and confuse you. By all means get as much information as you can to help you make the right decision.

I see you involved with money proposals, job applications, even contracts that need to be signed so remain clear-headed as much as possible.

Your business skills and clear and concise communication will be at the heart of your life in 2009.

Love and pleasure

Mercury, which rules the signs of Gemini and Virgo, will make your love life a little difficult due to its changeable nature. On the one hand you'll feel passionate and loving to your partner, yet on the other you will feel like giving it all up for the excitement of a new affair. Maintain the middle ground.

Also, try not to be too critical with your friends and family members. The influence of Virgo makes you prone to expecting much more from others than they're capable of giving. Control your sharp tongue and don't hurt people's feelings. Encouraging others is the better path, leading to more emotional satisfaction.

Work

Speed will dominate your professional life in 2009. You'll be flitting from one subject to another and taking on far more than you can handle. You'll need to make some serious changes in your routine to handle the avalanche of work that will come your way. You'll also be travelling with your work, but not necessarily overseas.

If you're in a job you enjoy then this year will give you additional successes. If not, it may be time to move on.

Improving your luck

Communication is the secret of attaining your desires in the coming twelve months. Keep focused on one idea rather than scattering your energies in all directions and your success will be speedier.

By looking after your health, sleeping well and exercising regularly, you'll build up your resilience and mental strength.

The 1st, 8th, 15th and 20th hours of Wednesday are lucky so it's best to schedule your meetings and other important social engagements during these times. The lucky numbers for Mercury are 5, 14, 23 and 32.

6 = Year of Venus

Overview

Because you're ruled by 6 this year, love is in the air! Venus, Taurus and Libra are well known for their affinity with romance, love, and even marriage. If ever you were going to meet a soulmate and feel comfortable in love, 2009 must surely be your year.

Taurus has a strong connection to money and practical affairs as well, so finances will also improve if you are diligent about work and security issues.

The important thing to keep in mind this year is that sharing love and making that important soul connection should be kept high on your agenda. This will be an enjoyable period in your life.

Love and pleasure

Romance is the key thing for you this year and your current relationships will become more fulfilling if you happen to be attached. For singles, a 6 year heralds an important meeting that eventually leads to marriage.

You'll also be interested in fashion, gifts, jewellery and all sorts of socialising. It's at one of these social engagements that you could meet the love of your life. Remain available!

Venus is one of the planets that has a tendency to overdo things, so be moderate in your eating and drinking. Try generally to maintain a modest lifestyle.

Work

You'll have a clearer insight into finances and your future security during a number 6 year. Whereas you may have had additional expenses and extra distractions previously, your mind will be more settled and capable of longer-term planning along these lines.

With the extra cash you might see this year, decorating your home or office will give you a special sort of satisfaction.

Social affairs and professional activities will be strongly linked. Any sort of work-related functions may offer you romantic opportunities as well. On the other hand, be careful not to mix up your workplace relationships with romantic ideals. This could complicate some of your professional activities.

Improving your luck

You'll want more money and a life of leisure and ease in 2009. Keep working on your strengths and eliminate your negative personality traits to create greater luck and harmony in your life.

Moderate all your actions and don't focus exclusively on money and material objects. Feed your spiritual needs as well. By balancing the inner and outer you'll see that your romantic and professional life will be enhanced more easily.

The 1st, 8th, 15th and 20th hours on Fridays will be very lucky for you and new opportunities will arise for you at those times. You can use the numbers 6, 15, 24 and 33 to increase luck in your general affairs.

7 = Year of Neptune

Overview

The last and most evolved sign of the zodiac is Pisces, which is ruled by Neptune. The number 7 is deeply connected with this zodiacal sign and governs you in 2009. Your ideals seem to be clearer and more spiritually orientated than ever before. Your desire to evolve and understand your inner self will be a double-edged sword. It depends on how organised you are as to how well you can use these spiritual and abstract concepts in your practical life.

Your past emotional hurts and deep emotional issues will be dealt with and removed for good, if you are serious about becoming a better human being.

Spend a little more time caring for yourself rather than others, as it's likely some of your friends will drain you of energy with their own personal problems. Of course, you mustn't turn a blind eye to the needs of others, but don't ignore your own personal needs in the process.

Love and pleasure

Meeting people with similar life views and spiritual aspirations will rekindle your faith in relationships. If you do choose to develop a new romance, make sure that there is a clear understanding of the responsibilities of one to the other. Don't get swept off your feet by people who have ulterior motives.

Keep your relationships realistic and see that the most idealistic partnerships must eventually come down to Earth. Deal with the practicalities of life.

Work

This is a year of hard work, but one in which you'll come to understand the deeper significance of your professional ideals. You may discover a whole new aspect to your career, which involves a more compassionate and self-sacrificing side to your personality.

You'll also find that your way of working will change and that you'll be more focused and able to get into the spirit of whatever you do. Finding meaningful work is very likely and therefore this could be a year when money, security, creativity and spirituality overlap to bring you a great sense of personal satisfaction.

Tapping into your greater self through meditation and self-study will bring you great benefits throughout 2009.

Improving your luck

Using self-sacrifice along with discrimination will be an unusual method of improving your luck. The laws of karma state that what you give, you receive in greater measure. This is one of the principal themes for you in 2009.

The 1st, 8th, 15th and 20th hours of Tuesdays are your lucky times. The numbers 7, 16, 25 and 34 should be used to increase your lucky energies.

8 = Year of Saturn

Overview

The earthy and practical sign of Capricorn and its ruler Saturn are intimately linked to the number 8, which rules you in 2009. Your discipline and farsightedness will help you achieve great things in the coming year. With cautious discernment, slowly but surely you will reach your goals.

It may be that due to the influence of the solitary Saturn, your best work and achievement will be behind closed doors away from the limelight. You mustn't fear this as you'll discover many new things about yourself. You'll learn just how strong you really are.

Love and pleasure

Work will overshadow your personal affairs in 2009, but you mustn't let this erode the personal relationships you have. Becoming a workaholic brings great material successes but will also cause you to become too insular and aloof. Your family members won't take too kindly to you working 100-hour weeks.

Responsibility is one of the key words for this number and you will therefore find yourself in a position of authority that leaves very little time for fun. Try to make time to enjoy the company of friends and family and by all means schedule time off on the weekends as it will give you the peace of mind you're looking for.

Because of your responsible attitude it will be very hard for you not to assume a greater role in your workplace and this indicates longer working hours with the likelihood of a promotion with equally good remuneration.

Work

Money is high on your agenda in 2009. Number 8 is a good money number according to the Chinese and this year is at last likely to bring you the fruits of your hard labour. You are cautious and resourceful in all your dealings and will not waste your hard-earned savings. You will also be very conscious of using your time wisely.

You will be given more responsibilities and you're likely to take them on, if only to prove to yourself that you can handle whatever life dishes up.

Expect a promotion in which you will play a leading role in your work. Your diligence and hard work will pay off, literally, in a bigger salary and more respect from others.

Improving your luck

Caution is one of the key characteristics of the number 8 and is linked to Capricorn. But being overly cautious could cause you to miss valuable opportunities. If an offer is put to you, try to think outside the square and balance it with your naturally cautious nature.

Be gentle and kind to yourself. By loving yourself, others will naturally love you, too. The 1st, 8th, 15th and 20th hours of Saturdays are exceptionally lucky for you as are the numbers 1, 8, 17, 26 and 35.

9 = Year of Mars

Overview

You are now entering the final year of a nine-year cycle dominated by the planet Mars and the sign of Aries. You'll be completing many things and are determined to be successful after several years of intense work.

Some of your relationships may now have reached their use-by date and even these personal affairs may need to be released. Don't let arguments and disagreements get in the road of friendly resolution in these areas of your life.

Mars is a challenging planet and, this year, although you will be very active and productive, you may find others trying to obstruct the achievement of your goals. As a result you may react strongly to them, thereby creating disharmony in your workplace. Don't be so impulsive or reckless, and generally slow things down. The slower, steadier approach has greater merit this year.

Love and pleasure

If you become too bossy and pushy with friends this year you will just end up pushing them out of your life. It's a year to end certain friendships but by the same token it could be the perfect time to end conflicts and thereby bolster your love affairs in 2009.

If you're feeling a little irritable and angry with those you love, try getting rid of these negative feelings through some intense, rigorous sports and physical activity. This will definitely relieve tension and improve your personal life.

Work

Because you're healthy and able to work at a more intense pace you'll achieve an incredible amount in the coming year. Overwork could become a problem if you're not careful.

Because the number 9 and Mars are infused with leadership energy, you'll be asked to take the reins of the job and steer your company or group in a certain direction. This will bring with it added responsibility but also a greater sense of purpose for you.

Improving your luck

Because of the hot and restless energy of the number 9, it is important to create more mental peace in your life this year. Lower the temperature, so to speak, and decompress your relationships rather than becoming aggravated. Try to talk to your work partners and loved ones rather than telling them what to do. This will generally pick up your health and your relationships.

The 1st, 8th, 15th and 20th hours of Tuesdays are the luckiest for you this year and, if you're involved in any disputes or need to attend to health issues, these times are also very good for the best results. Your lucky numbers are 9, 18, 27 and 36.

SAGITTARIUS

2009:
Your Daily Planner

Without leaps of imagination, or dreaming, we lose the excitement of possibilities. Dreaming, after all, is a form of planning.

—Gloria Steinem

There is a little-known branch of astrology called electional astrology, and it can help you select the most appropriate times for many of your day-to-day activities.

Ancient astrologers understood the planetary patterns and how they impacted on each of us. This allowed them to suggest the best possible times to start various important activities. Many farmers today still use this approach: they understand the phases of the Moon, and attest to the fact that planting seeds on certain lunar days produces a far better crop than planting on other days.

The following section covers many areas of daily life, and uses the cycles of the Moon and the combined strength of the other planets to work out the best times to start different types of activity.

So to create your own personal almanac, first select the activity you are interested in, and then quickly scan the year for the best months to start it. When you have selected the month, you can finetune your timing by finding the best specific dates. You can then be sure that the planetary energies will be in sync with you, offering you the best possible outcome.

Coupled with what you know about your monthly and weekly trends, the daily planner can be a powerful tool to help you capitalise on opportunities that come your way this year.

Good luck, and may the planets bless you with great success, fortune and happiness in 2009!

Starting activities

How many times have you made a new year's resolution to begin a diet or be a better person in your relationships? And how many times has it not worked out? Well, the reason may be partly that you started out at the wrong time! How successful you are is strongly influenced by the position of the Moon and the planets when you begin a particular activity. You could be more successful with the following activities if you start them on the days indicated.

Relationships

We all feel more empowered on some days than on others. This is because the planets have some power over us—their movement and their relationships to each other determine the ebb and flow of our energies. And our level of self-confidence and our sense of romantic magnetism play an important part in the way we behave in relationships.

Your daily planner tells you the ideal dates for meeting new friends, initiating a love affair, spending time with family and loved ones—it even tells you the most appropriate times for sexual encounters.

You'll be surprised at how much more impact you make in your relationships when you tune yourself in to the planetary energies on these special dates.

Falling in love/restoring love

During these times you could expect favourable energies to meet your soulmate or, if you've had difficulty in a relationship, to approach the one you love to rekindle both your and their emotional responses:

January	28, 30
February	25, 26
March	6, 7, 8, 28, 29, 30
April	25, 26, 30
May	1, 2, 5, 7, 26, 27, 28, 29

June	2, 3, 23, 24, 26, 29, 30
July	22, 23, 26, 27
August	14, 15, 16, 17, 22, 23, 24
September	10, 14, 16, 19, 20, 21
October	9, 10, 11, 12, 13
November	25, 26
December	22, 23, 27, 31

Special times with friends and family

Socialising, partying and having a good time with those you enjoy being with is highly favourable under the following dates. These dates are excellent to spend time with family and loved ones in a domestic environment:

January	26
February	8, 12, 13, 14, 22, 23, 24
March	8, 22, 23
April	19, 27, 28
May	1, 2, 15, 16, 17, 24, 25, 28, 29
June	2, 3, 11, 12, 13, 22, 30
July	23, 26, 27
August	5, 6, 23, 24
September	16
October	13
November	8, 10, 24
December	19, 20, 21, 29

Healing or resuming relationships

If you're trying to get back together with the one you love and need a heart-to-heart or deep and meaningful, you can try the following dates to do so:

February	8, 12, 13, 14
March	8
April	18, 19
May	1, 2, 28, 29
June	2, 3, 30
July	23, 26, 27
August	23, 24
September	16
October	13
November	8
December	22, 23, 27

Sexual encounters

Physical and sexual energies are well favoured on the following dates. The energies of the planets enhance your moments of intimacy during these times:

January	5, 30
February	25, 26
March	6, 7, 8, 28, 29, 30
April	25, 26, 30
May	1, 2, 5, 7, 26, 27, 28, 29
June	2, 3, 23, 24, 26, 29, 30

July	22, 23, 26, 27
August	23, 24
September	16
October	13
November	25, 26
December	22, 23, 27, 31

Health and wellbeing

Your aura and life force are susceptible to the movements of the planets; in particular, they respond to the phases of the Moon.

The following dates are the most appropriate times to begin a diet, have cosmetic surgery, or seek medical advice. They also tell you when the best times are to help others.

Feeling of wellbeing

Your physical as well as your mental alertness should be strong on these following dates. You can plan your activities and expect a good response from others:

January	8, 9, 26, 27
February	4, 5, 22, 23
March	31
April	18, 19, 27, 28
May	16, 17
June	21, 22
July	19
August	5, 6, 24, 25
September	12, 28, 30

October	8, 9
November	8, 10
December	19, 20, 21, 29, 30

Healing and medicine

This is good for approaching others who have expertise at a time when you need some deeper understanding. This is also favourable for any sort of healing or medication and making appointments with doctors or psychologists. Planning surgery around these dates should bring good results.

Often giving up our time and energy to assist others doesn't necessarily result in the expected outcome. By lending a helping hand to a friend on the following dates, the results should be favourable:

January	1, 20, 21, 22, 23, 24, 25, 26, 27, 28, 29, 30, 31
February	9, 10, 11, 12, 13, 14, 15, 16, 17, 18, 19, 20, 21, 22, 23, 24, 25, 26, 27, 28
March	2, 3, 4, 5, 6, 7, 8, 9, 22, 26, 28, 29, 30, 31
April	1, 10, 12, 15, 18, 20, 27, 28, 29, 30
May	1, 3, 7, 8, 9, 10, 11, 12
June	6, 7, 9, 13, 14, 15, 19, 21, 22
July	5, 6, 7, 8, 10, 12, 18, 19, 20, 25, 26
August	6, 7, 8, 9, 10, 29, 30, 31
September	1, 6, 27
October	8, 9, 10, 11, 12, 25, 26
November	18, 19, 20, 21, 22
December	10, 11, 12

Money

Money is an important part of life, and involves many decisions; decisions about borrowing, investing, spending. The ideal times for transactions are very much influenced by the planets, and whether your investment or nest egg grows or doesn't grow can often be linked to timing. Making your decisions on the following dates could give you a whole new perspective on your financial future.

Managing wealth and money

To build your nest egg, it's a good time to open your bank account and invest money on the following dates:

January	3, 4, 5, 10, 11, 16, 17, 23, 24, 25, 31
February	1, 6, 7, 12, 13, 14, 20, 21, 27, 28
March	5, 6, 7, 12, 13, 19, 26, 27
April	2, 3, 8, 9, 15, 17, 23, 24, 29, 30
May	5, 6, 7, 13, 14, 20, 21, 26, 27
June	2, 3, 9, 10, 16, 17, 18, 23, 24, 29, 30
July	6, 7, 8, 14, 15, 20, 21, 26, 27
August	2, 3, 4, 10, 11, 17, 18, 23, 24, 30, 31
September	6, 7, 13, 14, 19, 20, 26, 27
October	3, 4, 5, 10, 11, 16, 17, 18, 23, 24, 25, 31
November	1, 6, 7, 13, 14, 20, 21, 27, 28
December	4, 5, 10, 11, 17, 18, 24, 25, 26, 31

Spending

It's always fun to spend but the following dates are more in tune with this activity and are likely to give you better results:

January	20, 28, 30
February	3
March	28, 29, 30
April	25, 26
May	31
June	1, 2, 7, 8, 9, 10, 28, 30
July	1, 2, 3, 26, 27, 29, 30
August	2, 3, 4, 5, 20, 21, 22, 23, 24, 25
September	19, 20, 21, 22, 23
October	9, 10
November	1, 7, 8, 17
December	27, 28

Selling

If you're thinking of selling something, whether it is small or large, consider the following dates as ideal times to do so:

January	3, 18, 19, 20, 21, 25, 26, 27, 28, 29, 30, 31
February	8, 10, 11, 12, 13, 14, 15, 18, 20, 22, 23, 24, 26, 28
March	2, 3, 4, 5, 6, 7, 8, 9, 16, 26, 27, 28, 31
April	5, 10, 19, 20, 23, 25, 27, 28, 29
May	1, 2, 7, 9, 13, 14, 21, 24, 25, 28, 29, 31
June	1, 2, 7, 8, 14, 16, 17, 20, 21, 22, 26, 30
July	1, 2, 3, 9, 10, 11, 15, 16, 17, 26, 27
August	2, 3, 4, 13, 14, 15, 16, 17
September	1, 2, 3, 4, 5, 6, 14, 15, 16, 17, 21, 22, 23, 24, 25, 26, 27, 28, 30, 31

October	1, 2, 3, 4, 5, 6, 7, 8, 9, 10, 11, 12, 31
November	2, 3, 9, 10, 11, 12, 13, 25, 26, 27, 28, 29, 30
December	1, 2, 3, 7, 8, 9, 17, 20

Borrowing

Few of us like to borrow money, but if you must, taking out a loan on the following dates should be positive:

January	11, 18, 19, 20, 23, 24, 25
February	15, 16, 20, 21
March	14, 15, 19, 20
April	10, 11, 12, 15, 16, 17
May	9, 13, 14
June	9, 10
July	7, 8, 20, 21
August	17, 18
September	13, 14
October	10, 11
November	6, 7, 15, 16
December	4, 5, 12, 13, 14

Work and education

Your career is important to you, and continual improvement of your skills is therefore also crucial, professionally, mentally and socially. The dates below will help you find out the most appropriate times to improve your professional talents and commence new work or education associated with your work.

You may need to decide when to start learning a new skill, when to ask for a promotion, and even when to make an important career change. Here are the days when mental and educational power is strong.

Learning new skills

Educational pursuits are lucky and bring good results on the following dates:

January	8, 9
February	4, 5
March	3, 4, 10, 31
April	1, 6, 7, 27, 28
May	3, 4, 25, 30, 31
June	1, 6, 7, 27, 28
July	4, 5, 24, 25, 31
August	1, 21, 22, 27, 28, 29
September	23, 24, 25
October	21, 22
November	17, 18, 19
December	29, 30

Changing career path or profession

If you're feeling stuck and need to move into a new professional activity, changing jobs can be done at these times:

January	6, 7
February	2, 3
March	1, 2, 3, 4, 5, 6, 7, 8, 9, 10, 28, 29, 30
April	6, 7, 25, 26
May	3, 4, 30, 31
June	1, 27, 28

July	6, 24, 25
August	2, 3, 4, 21, 22, 30, 31
September	26, 27
October	23, 24, 25
November	2, 20, 21, 29, 30
December	1, 17, 18, 27, 28

Promotion, professional focus and hard work

To increase your mental focus and achieve good results from the work you do, promotions are likely on these dates that follow:

January	4, 5, 6, 11, 12, 13, 14, 15, 16, 21
February	6
March	18, 19, 20
April	8, 28, 29
May	12, 21
June	25, 26
July	1, 2, 3, 8, 15, 17
August	4, 14, 15, 16, 17, 18, 22, 23, 24
September	14, 15, 18, 19, 23, 24, 25, 26
October	22
November	7, 10, 11, 12, 17
December	1, 2, 3, 7, 28

Travel

Setting out on a holiday or adventurous journey is exciting. To gain the most out of your holidays and journeys, travelling on the following dates is likely to give you a sense of fulfilment:

January	9, 10, 28, 29, 30, 31
February	1, 4, 5, 26
March	3, 4, 5, 6, 7, 27, 31
April	27, 28, 29
May	1, 2, 25
June	6, 7, 25, 26
July	6, 31
August	1, 2, 21, 22, 23, 24, 29
September	19, 20, 23, 24, 25, 26, 27
October	1, 2, 3, 25, 28, 29, 30, 31
November	1, 17, 18, 26, 28
December	17, 18, 23, 26

Beauty and grooming

Believe it or not, cutting your hair or nails has a powerful effect on your body's electromagnetic energy. If you cut your hair or nails at the wrong time of the month, you can reduce your level of vitality significantly. Use these dates to ensure you optimise your energy levels by staying in tune with the stars.

Hair and nails

January	1, 2, 8, 9, 21, 22, 28, 29, 30
February	4, 5, 17, 18, 19, 25, 26
March	3, 4, 16, 17, 18, 24, 25, 31
April	1, 13, 14, 20, 21, 22, 27, 28, 29, 30
May	8, 10, 11, 12, 18, 19, 24, 25
June	6, 7, 8, 14, 15, 21, 22

July	4, 5, 11, 12, 13, 18, 19, 31
August	1, 7, 8, 9, 14, 15, 16, 27, 28, 29
September	4, 5, 11, 12, 23, 24, 25
October	1, 2, 8, 9, 21, 22, 28, 29, 30
November	4, 5, 17, 18, 19, 25, 26
December	2, 3, 15, 16, 22, 23, 29, 30

Therapies, massage and self-pampering

January	18, 19, 20, 26, 27
February	3, 6, 7, 8, 12, 13, 14, 15, 16, 22, 23, 24
March	6, 8, 28, 29, 30
April	5, 8, 9, 18, 19, 25, 26, 29, 30
May	1, 2, 5, 7, 9, 15, 16, 17, 22, 23, 26, 27, 28, 29
June	2, 3, 4, 5, 11, 12, 13, 19, 20, 23, 24, 26, 30
July	1, 2, 3, 9, 10, 23, 26, 27, 28, 29, 30
August	6, 12, 13, 17, 18, 19, 20, 23, 24, 25, 26
September	1, 2, 13, 14, 16
October	10, 11, 12, 13, 16, 17, 27
November	8, 9, 10, 13, 16, 23, 24, 29, 30
December	1, 4, 5, 6, 7, 10, 11, 12, 13, 14, 19, 20, 21, 27, 28, 31

MILLS & BOON®
Romance

Pure romance, pure emotion

4 brand-new titles each month

Available on the first Friday of every month
from WHSmith, ASDA, Tesco
and all good bookshops
www.millsandboon.co.uk

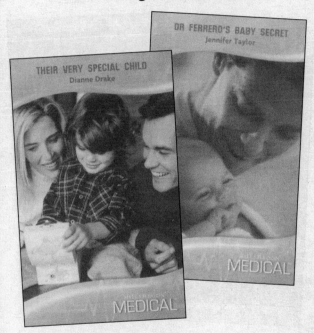

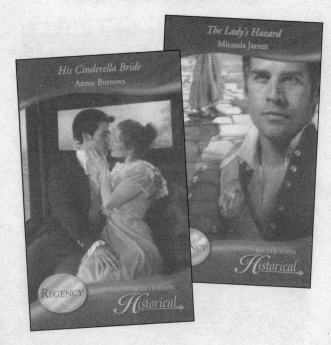

Life, love and family

6 brand-new titles each month

Available on the third Friday of every month
from WHSmith, ASDA, Tesco
and all good bookshops
www.millsandboon.co.uk

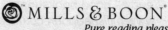